T3-BNW-603

THE EFFECT OF PRAISE AND
COMPETITION ON THE PERSISTING BEHAVIOR OF
KINDERGARTEN CHILDREN

UNIVERSITY OF MINNESOTA
THE INSTITUTE OF CHILD WELFARE
MONOGRAPH SERIES NO. XV

The Effect of
Praise and Competition on the
PERSISTING BEHAVIOR OF
KINDERGARTEN CHILDREN

BY

THETA HOLMES WOLF, Ph. D.

FORMERLY RESEARCH ASSISTANT
INSTITUTE OF CHILD WELFARE
UNIVERSITY OF MINNESOTA

GREENWOOD PRESS, PUBLISHERS
WESTPORT, CONNECTICUT

104447

Library of Congress Cataloging in Publication Data

Wolf, Theta Holmes, 1904-
  The effect of praise and competition on the persisting behavior of kindergarten children.

    Reprint of the ed. published by University of
Minnesota Press, Minneapolis, which was issued as
no. 15 of the University of Minnesota, Institute
of Child Welfare monograph series.
    Bibliography: p.
    Includes index.
    1. Rewards and punishments in education.
2. Praise. 3. Kindergarten. I. Title. II. Series: Minnesota. University. Institute of Child
Development and Welfare. Monograph series ; no. 15.
LB3025.W64 1975   372.1'5'3   76-141552
ISBN 0-8371-5899-0

Reprinted in 1975 by Greenwood Press, Inc.,
51 Riverside Avenue, Westport, Conn. 06880

Library of Congress catalog card number 76-141552

ISBN 0-8371-5899-0

Printed in the United States of America

10 9 8 7 6 5 4 3 2

FOREWORD

The author of this study faced several inter-related problems, and in the process of solving each of them she has made significant contributions. Examining the effect of praise and competition on the persisting behavior of five-year-old children, she had to evolve a satisfactory definition of such behavior, set up a practical and adequately controlled experiment for testing it, and interpret both her own findings and those of related studies in this comparatively unexplored field.

In formulating her definition, Mrs. Wolf presents a very useful analysis of the whole concept of persisting behavior. As she says, the value of several older studies has been limited by the failure of the investigators to go beyond their group data in their analyses. She attempts to point out those factors in both the momentary situation and in each child's permanent social field that seem to be related to the primary "goal activity" apparent in his pattern of persisting behavior. Thus she makes use of Lewin's "tension system" theories as points of departure or working tools rather than as finally accepted principles.

In her experimental setup, Mrs. Wolf devised some novel tasks that proved to be excellently adapted to the interests and abilities of her kindergarten subjects and to the incentives used. Important for our understanding of the effect of incentives is her finding that both the nature of the task and—in at least some instances—the order of its presentation in a series had a marked effect on persisting performance. In any future study in this field, her hypothesis that "the effect of each incentive is relative to the various stimulating conditions of which it is a part" will need to be taken into consideration. The numerous inter-relationships among the variables that seem to be associated with persisting behavior offer an attractive invitation for future students.

Worthy of particular attention is this author's detailed study of her individual subjects, from which she ascertained that the effect of incentives on persisting behavior may depend to some extent upon the subject's social milieu, his tendency to rationalize his failures, the conflict of his "tension systems," or other factors that vary markedly in different persons, even at five years of age.

Commendable caution is shown by Mrs. Wolf in drawing her conclusions. Her main finding is that persisting behavior in children appears to be the result "not of any single motive or need, but rather of a number of such needs, which may act to reinforce or to oppose the primary goal-directed activity of the organism." In other words, she concludes that "persisting behavior and the effect of incentives upon it are related to very pervasive aspects of personality."

Both in the special field of persisting behavior and motivation and in that of child psychology in general, this study is a valuable addition to the existing literature.

JOHN E. ANDERSON
Director, Institute of Child Welfare
University of Minnesota

ACKNOWLEDGMENTS

The writer wishes to express her indebtedness to the faculty and staff of the Institute of Child Welfare. She wishes especially to acknowledge the helpful assistance and suggestions of Dr. John E. Anderson, and the incisive criticism and generous counsel of Dr. Florence L. Goodenough, who directed the study.

T. H. W.

CONTENTS

THE EFFECT OF PRAISE AND COMPETITION ON THE PERSISTING BEHAVIOR OF KINDERGARTEN CHILDREN

I. THE PROBLEM

This investigation was undertaken in an attempt to examine the effect of several controlled variables on persisting behavior. It was frankly exploratory, planned with the purpose of varying a number of conditions to determine the direction of their influence. Several general problems must be considered in connection with persisting behavior and the effects of incentives upon it. It is important to discover whether persisting behavior, under varying conditions, is fundamentally a general or a specific reaction. That is to say, do the relations among the individuals in a group remain the same from one condition to another, or do these relations change with varying conditions? It is also desirable to study the records of persisting behavior in a number of individuals, in order to throw into relief some of the recurring individual variations. These must be accounted for if a satisfactory story of incentives and persisting behavior is to be written, and they are often lost —except as statistical measures of dispersion—in studies in which large numbers of subjects are used. It is important, too, to try to discover some of the reasons for the individual variations in persisting behavior.

Persisting behavior may be measured by the duration of time for which a subject works at any particular task with his interest and attention directed primarily to that task. In this study, brief fluctuations of the attention in response to other stimuli were not considered as affecting the persisting time. A persisting performance at any one task was considered ended when the subject left the task, dawdled at some phase of it for over a minute, or pursued some extraneous activity.

Five-year-olds were used as subjects. Each child was tested with five different tasks, and each task was repeated three times, with an essential variation in incentive for each repetition. Five different tasks were used, because there seemed to be reason for doubting the tacit assumption made by many previous investigators that the specific task has little or no bearing on responses to varying incentives. When this study was set up, a fundamental hypothesis of the experimenter was that, in any attempt to classify incentives as to relative degrees of effectiveness, certain qualifying variables must be considered, and that among them the kind of task and perhaps basic differences in the subjects' personality characteristics would be significant. It was a primary problem, then, to find group inter-relationships among the three following variables: kind of task, nature of incentive, and individual differences as exhibited in sex, intelligence quotients, socio-economic status, and age.

Because this was to be a study in a comparatively unexplored field of psychology, the writer was disinclined to give the problem an aspect of oversimplification. She proceeded on a further hypothesis that differences in persisting behavior and in response to incentives may be related to factors not only in the momentary situation, but also in the more permanent environment. She therefore collected from teachers and parents data which might provide suggestive hints for future quantitative investigation.

It will be evident that there has also been a conscious attempt in this experiment to find a measure of the intrinsic appeal of the task itself, apart from the appeal of the incentive situation. This would provide at least a rough measure of the effect of incentives. In previous experiments there has been little attempt, except in the determination of efficiency levels in well-formed habits, to differentiate between the intrinsic appeal of the task and some end to be gained by response to the incentive.

II. PREVIOUS EXPERIMENTS IN THE FIELD

ATTENDING BEHAVIOR

Experiments in persisting or attending behavior with preschool subjects have become fairly numerous in the last half-decade. They have been variously called studies in *attention span, interest span, perseverative tendency, persistence,* and *perseverance.*

The functional term *persisting behavior* is used in the present investigation to avoid classifying the phenomenon as though it had an essential nature apart from the conditions affecting it. The *activity* of the organism is best expressed by a *process* term. The way is then indicated toward a concept of functional variables of which this activity of the organism is a part.

In earlier studies the definition and nature of attention was of fundamental importance and the experimentation was carried out with adult subjects. The aspects of attention that interested psychologists were those concerned with brief fluctuations of sensory clearness or high degrees of sensorimotor adjustment to a highly particularized stimulus. This literature was summarized by Geissler in 1909 (13) and again by Dallenbach in 1928 (10). Dallenbach included only one experiment in which preschool subjects were used—that of Bertrand, which is summarized in this chapter.

Although there have been a few ingenious studies, with preschool children as subjects, of what we may call the "classical" aspects of attention—those of Taylor (41), Poyntz (37), and Miles (32), for example—on the whole such topics were not applicable to young children. Under the aegis of behavior and process psychology, however, and with the extension of observational studies, the concept of attention has been broadened to include *activity span.* This implies a more generally oriented activity, differing from the former concept primarily in the degree of sensorimotor and inhibitory adjustment of the organism and in the specificity with which the stimulus field is defined. The duration of an activity, rather than the speed of reaction or the fluctuation of attentive consciousness, becomes the measurement unit.

Observational studies of the attending behavior of preschool children in natural free-play situations generally preceded con-

5

trolled experiments. These observational studies measured the duration of children's voluntary preoccupation with different materials in a group situation. Since Shacter (39) has summarized these studies, they will not be treated in this survey. The eight more or less controlled studies that follow belong in a review of preschool studies of attention, but they are not similar enough to the present study to warrant detailed accounts.

In 1925 Bertrand (2) studied the chronological development of attention by measuring the length of time that children from two to six years of age, alone with the experimenter, devoted to a single toy chosen voluntarily from among several. He found an increase of attention span with age. In 1930 Herring and Koch (19) made a somewhat similar study, except that they allowed each child to take any number of toys he desired, and timed his occupation with each one. These experimenters also found a slight increase in the interest span with age and a slight sex difference in favor of the boys, but there was no evidence of consistent variations according to the intelligence test quotient or the time of day. The mean time spent at a single task was one and one-half to two and one-half minutes. The experimenters indicate some important causes of unreliability in their data.

In 1930 Brown (5) made a study of continuous discrimination-reaction among five-year-olds. He found that the final level of achievement appeared to be a function of the ability to distribute attention over a field. He felt that this ability was less dependent on intelligence than on factors of emotional stability.

Taylor in 1931 (41) published a comparative study of the span of visual apprehension in nursery school children and college students, using as her materials animal toys and other inanimate objects. The mean span for the children included about four fewer objects than that for the adults, and the children made poorer scores in the later trials, whereas the adults improved with practice. The children's scores showed a high correlation with chronological and mental age.

Leontiev (25), studying children aged five and six, older children, and adults, posited the development of voluntary from involuntary attention. Answers to a series of questions were limited by "forbidding" certain responses and were supposedly facilitated by external stimuli by which the subjects' behavior could be organized. Children of preschool age "prove incapable of actively using external auxiliary stimuli" to organize their behavior, and

Leontiev concluded therefore that they are incapable of voluntary attention.

Miles (32) studied the sustained visual fixation to a delayed stimulus of children aged from two years six months to six years three months. The time was measured during which a child kept his eyes fixed upon the spot where an anticipated stimulus was to appear. The stimulus was delayed by the experimenter until the child's eyes wandered. Sex differences were negligible, and there was no relation with intelligence test scores. With chronological age, however, the relation was close.

The relative effectiveness of visual and auditory distractions upon the performance of a standard task by preschool children was studied by Poyntz (37). The visual distractions proved more effective than the auditory. Individual differences were not reliably associated with any of the factors studied.

Bestor (3) recently attempted a study of attention, which she says is specifically and limitedly defined by Dashiell as "the attitude facilitating the response of an individual to some particular stimulus or stimuli." Desiring "meaningless" visual and auditory experimental stimuli, she used for the former a "light shining behind an irregular, opaque field about two feet in area," and flashing intermittently. The auditory stimulus was the Seashore test for musical pitch discrimination. The child's attention span was the length of time he stayed within an area in which he *could* see the light, or in the room where the record was being played. A positive but very low relationship was found between the visual and auditory scores. Bestor gave her subjects samples of Shacter's (39) and Cushing's (9) materials and found low relationships between her material and theirs. It is fair to suggest that obviously Dashiell's definition applies as well to a meaningful activity span as to Bestor's material. Unfortunately for her purpose and also for her claim, her "meaningless" stimuli brought forth many interested comments from the children concerning their nature and origin. Bestor quotes these comments frankly, but fails to note that they imply something much more than a simple sensory response to meaningless material. Indeed, the reader is left in considerable doubt as to the nature of the process that was measured.

The next three studies are reported in greater detail, because they deal with a kind of behavior very much like that studied in the present investigation, and they will later be intercompared with the group results of the present study. The reader should not be misled by the fact that these studies are variously called investigations of *perseverative tendency, persistence, sustained attention,* and *persisting behavior.* The description of the behavior processes observed indicates their fundamental similarity. The methods of investigation vary, however, and only in the present study was the factor of different incentives experimentally introduced.

Palmer (34) made a very early study of persistence, which she defined as "the keeping at a given task in the face of obstacles . . . an inner compulsion as opposed to anything external." Her subjects were from two to five and one-half years old. Twenty of them were in the age range of the present investigation. Palmer attempted to reduce motivation to the lowest degree, except as it appeared in a natural interest in the problem, but she realized that the factor of children's docility toward an adult's request affected the results. The children worked singly in the presence of the experimenter. One weakness in the control of the experiment was its being left to the experimenter to decide "when a child gave a clear sign of wanting to give up."

Palmer's tasks were of four kinds: bead-stringing, perforation, wire puzzle, and box puzzle. In the bead-stringing blue wooden beads were to be strung on red cord; an upper limit of two hundred and fifty beads was set. For the perforation task sixty pictures of girls' faces were mimeographed on a page, with eyes and mouth prepared for perforation with a stylus; an upper limit of five pages was set. In the first puzzle the task was to disengage two pieces of wire. Unfortunately for the persistence score, five children solved this puzzle. The second puzzle was a box containing a ball in plain sight, but a string had to be manipulated in order to open the box to reach the ball. Four children solved this puzzle. The writer has computed the median scores for the children in Palmer's group who were within the age range of the children in the present study. These medians are shown in Table 1.

The correlations between time scores on the various tasks for thirty-nine subjects ranged from $.17 \pm .06$ to $.35 \pm .09$, with an average of .27. On the basis of partial Pearson coefficients, chronological and mental age did not appear to be factors in the individual differences. The boys showed a slightly lower mean score than the girls, but the amount of overlapping was not determined.

Cushing (9) called the activity that she measured *perseverative tendency.* Her criterion of performance was the time during which the subjects spontaneously manipulated the material without pausing longer than one minute. Like Palmer, however, she was always present, and did not tell the subject that he could leave when he wished. In her choice of materials she attempted to reduce the

TABLE 1.—MEDIAN MANIPULATION TIME FOR FOUR TASKS
IN PALMER'S STUDY

TASK	DURATION (MINUTES)	QUARTILE DEVIATION
Bead-stringing	25.5	12.5
Perforation test	14.5	4.0
Wire puzzle	2.5	1.6
Box puzzle	10.7	4.0

goal appeal in all but one task, a lock-and-key puzzle which she considered the single test of *persistence.* Her task of dropping marbles through a hole in a box was similar to the ball-dropping task in the present experiment. She gave the children one material at a trial. There were seventy children, aged from twenty-three to sixty months, only four being as old as those in the present

TABLE 2.—MEAN MANIPULATION TIME FOR SIX TASKS IN CUSHING'S STUDY

TASK	MINUTES	SIGMAS
Dropping marbles	20.1	12.6
Auditory stimuli (two kinds of bells, a whistle, and a snapper) .	15.9	8.7
Visual stimulus (mechanical "star-making" machine)	9.6	5.1
Nest of boxes.	17.9	10.0
Motor toys.	21.1	11.0
Lock-and-key puzzle.	3.3	3.2

study. The experimenter was not only present, but she encouraged and urged on the child's activity during the first minute of the test. This minute was counted in the perseverative time, a condition not operative in the other studies in this group. The average manipulation times for the whole group are shown in Table 2.

If the lock-and-key puzzle is omitted (although this was considered a test of persistence, it gave by far the lowest average score) the intercorrelations between scores on the various tasks ranged from .18±.08 to .61±.05, with an average of .42. With mental age held constant, the correlation of chronological age with the composite scores was only .008. With chronological age held constant, mental age showed the positive but negligible correlation of .28. The scores were also little influenced by sex or socio-economic status, although the boys slightly exceeded the girls. On the basis of the tetrad-difference formula, Cushing states that there is evidence of the presence of a common factor plus small group factors in occupations of young children that involve manipulative materials of "a simple repetitive sort."

Shacter (39) presented her materials in practically the same manner as Cushing. Her study is interesting for its comparative performances on simple and complex aspects of the same sort of tasks. Her three tasks seem, to an adult at least, essentially similar. All consisted of some sort of placing or matching activity. Her subjects were three-, four-, and five-year-olds, twelve at each age level, equally divided according to sex. Her definition of attention span is essentially the same as the definition of persisting behavior in the present study and of perseverative tendency in Cushing's study. At the five-year age level the average span was 9 minutes 22 seconds (mean deviation 3 minutes 15 seconds) for the simple tasks and 11 minutes 14 seconds (mean deviation 3 minutes 45 seconds) for the complex. Age was not found to be a factor in the average spans. The girls had a longer span than the boys by about 1.5 minutes on the simple, 2.5 minutes on the complex, tasks. There were, however, no data on the percentage of overlapping, nor any giving the intercorrelations between the task performances.

In two separate studies Shacter has examined intelligence and extroversion-introversion as causal factors in the individual differences of her subjects. In studying the effect of intelligence (38) she used a composite score from three tests: the Stanford-Binet, the Merrill-Palmer, and the Detroit Kindergarten. The product-moment r's, converted from rank-difference coefficients, are .12±.12 between the average test scores and the simple tasks and .33±.10 between the scores and the complex tasks. At each age level, considered separately, the r's are higher between the complex tasks and the intelligence test score than between the simple tasks and the test score. They also show a tendency to decrease in size as age increases, which "may indicate a very definite relationship between the significance of material and the length of time the subjects will attend."

Shacter's measure for introversion-extroversion (40) was the familiar Marston rating scale (31), on which she had ratings for the thirty-six children. The r's are again Pearsonian coefficients converted from rank-difference coefficients. The correlation for the simple situations with the ratings was .67±.07 and for the complex .74±.05. Shacter's conclusion, drawn with well-expressed caution, is that "extrovertive characteristics are associated with a short attention span, and introvertive . . . with a long attention span." Certainly this is a higher correlation than has ever been approached with sex, age, or intelligence, but it hardly justifies putting introversion-extroversion in the category of cause, as Shacter does in her hypothesis that "the underlying fundamental cause of the differing attentive behavior of the preschool subjects examined lies in personality differences." It is as plausible to assume a common cause for introversion and sustained attention as to assume that one is a "necessary antecedent condition" to the other.

These studies show no agreement on sex differences. In duration of activity span, Bertrand, Palmer, and Shacter found the girls' average scores a little higher than the boys', while Herring and Koch and Cushing found a slight advantage for the boys. In sustained visual fixation Miles found the difference negligible, and Poyntz's results indicate that susceptibility to distractions is uninfluenced by sex. As Shacter suggests, the sex differences that were indicated may be accounted for by the nature of the experiment materials. It is possible, too, that the samplings, or even the treatment of the data, were responsible for the differences indicated.

Bertrand and Herring and Koch found an increase in time scores with chronological age, but their results have not been carefully analyzed. Bestor, Palmer, Cushing, and Shacter did not find that age is a factor related to the individual differences. Again, this finding may be due to the materials used. In order to be within the range of ability of the younger children, the tasks may be outside the interest range of the older ones. Age was found to have a close relation with span of apprehension (Taylor) and sustained visual fixation (Miles) but not with distractibility (Poyntz).

The intelligence quotient or mental age shows, in most cases, either no relationship to the behavior observed in these studies or a positive but negligible one. In the activity-span studies, Shacter found a low positive relation between intelligence quotient and the complex aspects of her tasks. No relationship was found between distractibility or sustained visual fixation and intelligence quotient.

Only between span of apprehension and mental age was a high relationship indicated.

Cushing and Poyntz, reporting on socio-economic status, indicate that it has little or no influence upon attention span or upon distractibility. In the studies reporting intercorrelations between tasks the coefficients are positive but, on the whole, not high. The average durations of manipulation are not strictly comparable, because the investigators were using different age groups and different materials. Durations range, however, from ten to twenty minutes, with the exception of those recorded by Herring and Koch. Here the children were free to change from one occupation to another, so that the average span was exceptionally brief.

It is clear that, while some special aspects of attention seem to be related to chronological age, the wide individual differences in persisting behavior shown in these experimental studies are not wholly accounted for by age or by the other factors usually studied. In Brown's study we find that the concentrated behavior necessary to efficient continuous discrimination-reactions may be associated with stabilized emotional behavior, and in Shacter's that sustained attention upon the manipulation of a single task may be associated with behavior called introverted. The next problem, then, is to discover what conditioning variables, within the stimulus field of the individual, are functionally related to these mutually associated behavior processes.

Karsten (24), studying the process of satiation for an activity, examined a behavior process not unrelated to that in the activity-span studies, and has indicated what some of these conditioning variables may be. Several different tasks were used, and although the subject was free to stop as soon as he had had enough of any task, the experimenter exerted a "weak pressure" toward his continuance. In one task the subject was to make strokes in a certain rhythm. When he would go no further in one rhythm he was asked to continue in another. This was repeated until he could not be induced to go on at all. The speed of satiation, which was determined by the time that the subject took to arrive at the point of final refusal to continue, was found to depend, among other things, "upon the structure of the task, upon the state of tension of the whole person, upon whether the task involved is of a more peripheral or more central character . . . , upon the character of the person." In the present study we shall be interested in searching for some of the functional variables in the stimulus field, in both the momentary and the more permanent aspects, that are related to individual differences in an unrestricted, voluntary manipulation of materials.

An introduction to the study of attending behavior among older children may be found in the studies of Philip (35 and 36), Crutcher (8), and Hartshorne, May, and Maller (17).

INCENTIVES AND THE PRESCHOOL CHILD

The subject of motivation and incentives has earned experimental significance in the study of the preschool child only within the last five or six years. For older children, adults, and animals there is, however, a large literature, which Diserens and Vaughn (11) summarized in 1931. They report few experiments in which older children were used as subjects and none in which the preschool child was studied. Bills has reviewed the topic of incentives and motives (4, chapters 12, 25, 26) more recently, and he too has ignored the preschool child. In Young (45), however, the reader will find summaries of studies in human motivation ranging from the young preschool child to the adult.

Most incentive and motivation studies in human psychology deal with learning, with the effect of motivation upon accuracy of the discriminative process, and especially with quantitative (and sometimes qualitative) aspects of performances involving the efficient use of habits already formed. These activities are difficult to control in the preschool child, perhaps because time limits are imposed; to the average preschool child a time limit is a meaningless stimulus. Measures of the voluntary duration of activity would seem, therefore, to offer a more satisfactory tool for the study of incentives among young children. Up to the present time this aspect of activity has been only very slightly examined. The amount of strength exerted under different incentive conditions has been used as a measure, but this has a very limited scope, as we shall observe in Chase's study described below.

Greenberg (16), working under C. Bühler at Vienna, did a pioneer study of competition in children aged two to seven years. Two children at a time, chosen indiscriminately with regard to sex, age, and home background, were set at the same table and each presented with small blocks. The experimenter spurred them to competition by suggesting that they see who could build the prettier block structure. The behavior, attitudes, and conversation of each child in relation to the materials and to the other child were recorded. The percentage of children exhibiting a reaction to the competition stimulus increased with each age level. The experimenter concluded that competition becomes a real stimulus at about four years of age. In addition, she deduced two general principles: first, that reaction to competition develops consistently with the child's mastery of the material, and second, that reaction to competition seems to be a human inclination that is nurtured and directed by education. Neither principle should properly be deduced on the basis of Greenberg's experiment. The first is tantamount only to repeating that the competitive impulse develops with chronological age, since both the attitude of rivalry and the ability to handle materials develop thus. Greenberg did not, moreover, make comparisons within an age range limited to such an extent that age would be held approximately constant. Her second principle is based upon the slight evidence that after the experimenter's suggestion there was a spurt in energy and competition. Of course, this could be more logically accounted for on the basis of temporary suggestibility rather than education. Greenberg states that there was a close relationship between the competitive impulse and the "instinct of pugnacity."

This observation on the relation between personality traits is confirmed by a very brief study of the relation of ascendancy to the competitive attitude by Jack (23). She set up an experimental situation to test the degree of ascendancy in young children. The children were brought to the experiment room in pairs to play with various materials in a sand box. The experimenter, watching from a concealed position, recorded the behavior interactions of the two children. The observational periods were five minutes in length. On the basis of scores derived from pairings of ten different children each child was given an ascendancy score based on the child's "attempts to pursue [his] own interests when they conflict with those of others, and to direct the behavior of [his] competitors" so that the latter would comply. With this experimental score the upper and lower thirds of a group of eighteen four-year-olds were chosen and observed in other play activities. Jack concludes that "expressions of a rivalrous, competitive attitude occurred twice as frequently in the ascendant group as in the nonascendant group." Presumably the ascendant group would be comparable with those showing the "instinct of pugnacity" in Greenberg's study. The apparent relationship of these behavior characteristics gives point to the real problem of the common basis for their association.

Leuba (26) independently set up a study very similar to Greenberg's but better controlled. His subjects were twenty-six children two to five years of age. Each child was given a preliminary five-minute trial alone with the material. A week later he was paired with another child partly on the basis of age, partly on that of the number of pegs he had put in a pegboard when he worked with only the experimenter present. Notes on rivalry responses indicated that the two-year-olds showed little response to the other child, while the three- and four-year-olds showed a variety of responses, including a few rivalry responses, but also a lessened output. Among the five-year-olds rivalry was usually dominant and output materially increased. Leuba states that his results tend to confirm Greenberg's so far as the two are comparable, but that his experiment differs from Greenberg's in that he tested his subjects alone with the pegboard material first, as a partial basis for pairing; that his materials yielded quantitative results; and that he made no attempt to promote rivalry. He makes the pertinent suggestion that case studies to discover the genesis of rivalry responses would be valuable.

Chase (7) introduced a series of failure and success incentives to a group of two hundred and fourteen children from two to eight years of age. The task she used was a hand dynamometer ingeniously constructed so that the experimenter could regulate the subject's apparent success or failure, but at the same time obtain a reading in kilogram units of the actual pressure exerted. This reading was used as the measure of the effects of the various incentives. The subjects were divided into four groups equated largely by chance. Each subject was tested three times in approximately three weeks. At each test period the subjects were given seven trials, the score being the average of the last six trials. Group A, the controls, were allowed merely a repetition performance each time, with no knowledge of results. Those in the other groups were all given this same "control motivation" the first time. Group B at the second testing was given success alone (ringing the bell) and on the third test failure alone. Group C was praised for success at the second testing and reproved for failure the third time. Group D was rewarded with a gold star for each success the second time and "punished" by having a button cut off a paper gingerbread doll for each failure at the third test. In the success series a bulb dynamometer showed the subjects their progress by a rising stream of water. In the failure group Chase used a train dynamometer which the subjects could see moving through an arc. In an effort to have the conditions as well controlled as possible, Chase went to the trouble of getting strobophotographic records of her voice to check her inflections in praise and reproof.

Differences in the results for the various incentive groups were in most cases not statistically significant, but in general the failure incentives were found to be more effective than the success incentives in raising dynamometer scores. Chase points out the three following factors which may have influenced her results: all the failure incentives were preceded by success incentives; the train dynamometer, used throughout the failure series, may have been more interesting than the water dynamometer used throughout the success series; and the "punishment" was not experienced as punishment by many subjects—indeed, some of them enjoyed seeing the gingerbread boy lose his buttons. Although Chase notes this fact herself, she goes on to draw her conclusions in accordance with her arbitrary classification. Since the situation has been called punishment, the resulting behavior is the effect of punishment!

Since Chase was very meticulous in her mechanical constructions, it seems surprising that she was comparatively careless in controlling some of the psychological conditions. She might at least have reversed the success and failure order for half the group, and also the use of the two types of dynamometers. It would also have been possible, with a small pre-experimental group, to have determined whether her choice of punishment was actually a psychological punishment for children of the various age levels. Her groups, too, should have been matched in some systematic order. This tremendous piece of work, moreover, included practically no analysis of individual differences. We know only that all the incentive situations used in the experiment were better than no incentive (which is not surprising in view of other experimental evidence), and that, under conditions which may easily have vitiated even the results indicated, failure incentives appeared to be more effective than success incentives in making children press harder on a dynamometer. Chase's results cannot be generalized beyond this, and she has given us no understanding whatever of the conditions that seem to have been significant in determining the effectiveness of the incentives she used.

Anderson and Smith (1) retested all Chase's subjects who were available three years later. Unfortunately this sampling included a disproportionate number of the older children and of the boys.

The later experimenters reproduced as exactly as possible Chase's procedure and technique, with the necessary modification of adding a heavy coil spring to the dynamometer apparatus to increase the tension on the levers so that the task would be sufficiently difficult for the oldest children. As in the Chase study, tension was regulated according to the child's first trial, which was not counted in the results. In all three series the children were given retests in the same motivation group in which they had originally been placed by Chase. The variability coefficients were lower in the retests than in the original tests for the same group. The same general results were found for the comparison of success and failure incentives, except that there were more approaches to significant differences in the Anderson-Smith data. No correlations between original and retest performances were given.

Fajans (12) studied the after-effects of success and failure in the behavior of infants from six to twelve months old and of children from two years to six years four months old. An inviting object (a doll or a chocolate) was placed before or above the child at varying distances, first near by, then farther away, and then near again. Each trial lasted four minutes for the children, three for the infants, with a five-minute rest interval between trials. All trials ended in failure, since attainment of the goal object was not permitted. Although the first and third conditions were objectively the same, yet the results indicate that for both groups the duration of approach (*Zuwendungsdauer*) in the second near trial was very much reduced.

To determine the effect of three repeated success trials with the goal object always at the same distance from the subject, one group on each age level was given three successsive near trials (18 centimeters for the children, 10 centimeters for the infants), and each trial was made to end in success. Different groups were given a similar series of three failure trials. For the older children the success trials gave approaches of progressively longer duration (from 88 to 110 seconds), the failure trials successively shorter approaches (from 75 to 40 seconds). For the infants even the success trials decreased (from 81 to 51 seconds), but the failure trials decreased more (from 74 to 12 seconds). This study, although based on a small number of subjects, suggests that failure and success may bring about significant changes in response in both infants and young children, and that the changes may be psychologically different for the two age groups.

In the following studies the effects of incentives are usually observed incidentally to another main problem. Two early studies of attitudes of rivalry among infants and preschool children in natural situations were made in Vienna.* Bühler and her fellow workers put together two children of varying age relations but both less than one year old, and gave a toy to one. The conclusion is that during the first half-year the child shows no rivalry, but that rivalry is "vigorously developed" during the second half-year. In this case rivalry and aggressiveness seem to be regarded as synonymous. Only children of approximately the same age (maximal difference of about two and one-half months) rival each other, and the older is almost always the despot. Hetzer observed that rivalry or competitive play in groups of children is absent before the age of three years. But between three and six years eight per cent of all the child's play is competitive.

Moore (33), in one part of a study of various aspects of mental health, gave her subjects a glass box to open by manipulating brass screws. Most of the children did not make so great an effort when the toys were removed from the box as when they were there.

CONCLUSIONS

We may conclude that, on the average, competition responses appear between the ages of four and five years, but we do not know anything about the consistency or strength of the competitive attitude. We have as yet no studies of the process, of its development, of the factors that are functionally related to the differences between individuals or to the differences in the same individual when psychological changes are apparent in the stimulus field or in his needs.

It seems patent that the value to psychological understanding of most of the studies reported above—studies both of attending behavior and incentive effects—is limited because the investigators have failed to go further in their analyses than their limited group data take them. Studies in which the group data represent valid categories offer significant suggestions of inter-relationships. But in their failure to look for the relationships that function for the in-

---

* These two studies are reported from Greenberg (16) who gives the references as follows: C. Bühler, H. Hetzer, and B. Tudor-hart, *Soziologische und psychologische Studien über das erste Lebensjahr* (Fischer, Jena, 1927), pp. 1–102; H. Hetzer, "Das volkstümliche Kinderspiel," *Wiener Arbeit. f. päd. Psychol.*, 6:75 (1927); and *Deutscher Verlag für Jugend und Volk* (Wien, 1927), p. 84. These references were not available to the writer.

dividual in the "total situation," the experimenters usually fail to get a hint of the many factors basic to an understanding of fundamental relationships. It is obvious that only an approximation can be made to a study of the "structure of the total situation," but even in a limited field-area significant conditions can be found. In the present study the writer has attempted to point out the negative and the positive factors in the momentary situation which were related—or appeared, on the basis of the behavior pattern, to be related—to the primary "goal activity" that oriented the child's behavior. In addition to this, she has attempted to discover in the more permanent social field factors that seemed to be related to the subject's attitudes and to the general state of tension apparent in his pattern of persisting behavior.

In putting so much value upon her "individual case" approach to the study of the present problem, the writer is not supporting Lewin's theory (28, chapter 1) of the validity of the single case to establish laws.* She is, rather, protesting against the oversimplification of the problem as it has appeared in many investigations. She uses the analyses of the single cases primarily to indicate the complexity of the variables that function in the behavior investigated, thereby pointing out some of the conditions that must be systematically varied in any experimental study of the behavior.

* Cf. Margineanu (30) for a critique of Lewin's concept.

III. THE EXPERIMENTAL SETUP

PROBLEMS INVOLVED

In the present experiment it was necessary to limit the choice of tasks, incentives, and subjects by certain considerations. It seemed advisable to vary not only the kind of task falling roughly within a single type, but also the types of tasks. The reason for this lies in the hypothesis already stated that the effect of the incentive is altered by the nature of the task that is being performed. An attempt was made to find one task that would be a difficult, problem-solving, construction task, in which the subject could easily see his own progress. Although this type of task does not offer so great a degree of performance control as the more commonly used puzzles, this difficulty seemed to be offset by the appeal of the task selected and by its consisting of a more natural play material.

Another type of task was to require a large-muscle motor skill, in which success would be limited but apparent to the subject. A third task was to require a finely coordinated skill, with no definite goal, but in which the subject could, if he wished, set a self-appointed goal for his performance. The fourth task was to be an automatic one, designed to have little intrinsic appeal although giving the subject some opportunity to note his progress. The fifth task was also to be automatic and even less attractive than the fourth; all visual clues to progress were to be excluded, and the material was to be colorless and lacking in imaginative appeal.

There were other limitations. The materials chosen had to be novel, or at least have novel elements in them, so as to minimize the effects of the subjects' previous experience. In order to ensure this condition either original tasks had to be constructed or original uses of familiar material devised. The manipulation of the materials had to be within the understanding of the subjects. Each task had to be of such a kind that the supplies for carrying it on could be easily accessible to the subject and inexhaustible enough to satisfy the most persistent. In the case of the construction task, the problem had to be of such complexity that no subject could complete it, and yet not so difficult as to discourage attempts to solve it. This providing of an endless task was absolutely necessary because, after the first introduction to any material, the subjects were expected to work without assistance from the experimenter. Since each task was to be presented three times, once for each of the three incentives, tasks must be found that could be varied in some particular from one situation to another to avoid monotony. And finally, material must be chosen in which the practice effect would be minimal, at least after a preliminary practice period which would be the same for each subject.

The choice of incentives was somewhat arbitrary. Praise and competition were chosen because they have been widely used in other experiments of various kinds and would, therefore, offer the basis for some rough comparisons; also, they appeared more satisfactory for an experiment with small children than most of the other possible incentives. An attempt was made to set up the incentive situations so that they would be objectively constant for all subjects. It will be shown later that this was more successful in the praise incentive than in competition. Finally, it was necessary to arrange one situation in which there was no incentive except that of the material itself, so that the effect of the incentives could be estimated apart from the "pull" of the tasks.

THE SUBJECTS

The subjects were twenty children from the kindergarten of the University of Minnesota, sixteen from the morning and four from the afternoon session. There were eleven girls, with an average IQ of 114; and nine boys, with an average IQ of 116. The parents' socio-economic status was determined by means of the Minnesota scale for paternal occupations (14), which assumes that each of the occupational groups makes progressively fewer demands on mental ability. There were six subjects in Group I, four in Group II, five in Group III, three in Group IV, and two in Group V. The chronological ages ranged from four years nine months to six years, with a median age of five years five months. The age of each child was computed to the first date on which the experimental material was presented to him.

The use of children rather than adults as subjects made it easier to limit the number of uncontrolled factors. Special interests and talents are not so highly developed or so exclusively absorbing in five-year-olds as they are in the older child or adult. It is more feasible, therefore, to find materials to which there is a fairly homogeneous type of interest response for five-year-olds than it would be for ten- or for thirty-year-olds. Moreover, young children's incentives to prolonged activity are probably simpler and more determinable than those of older persons. Their interests are not yet grouped around a lifework, or even around events a month or a week in advance, so that their activity of the moment is not influenced by motives as complex as those of adults. Presumably, also, sex differences due to social customs have not become habitually motivating at the age of five, so that any such differences found to exist may come less from environmental influences than from native disposition. Young children, too, usually lack sophistication toward incentives or motivating devices; they usually take the experimental setup naïvely, so that their behavior is not influenced by self-consciousness toward the conditions. Finally, young children, particularly in kindergarten or nursery school groups, are more available than older ones for daily or bi- and tri-weekly periods of experimentation, and they provide a less selected group than the college students who perform in many adult studies.

THE EXPERIMENTAL SITUATION

The experiment room was just across the hall from the kindergarten. It had a floor plan that easily allowed the use of a one-way screen to conceal the experimenter after the task to be done without further incentive had been presented to the child. The screen and the lighting arrangement were devised in such a way that the experimenter could not be seen from the subject's position when she sat behind the screen at a small table while watching and recording the subject's performance.

Experimental materials.—One of the tasks was the construction of a Tinker Toy model. A different model—a windmill, a steam shovel, or a derrick—was used for each of the three situations in which this task was performed, in order to lessen the effects of learning from one performance to the next. The models were of approximately equal difficulty. They had very similar basic construction patterns, there were from fifty to fifty-five pieces in each model, and each was equipped with a pulley arrangement so complicated that it would be impossible for any child to finish the task. The subjects were to copy the models with Tinker Toy pieces provided for them in an easily accessible box, which had compartments to fit the various pieces so that the subject could readily find and take out any piece. With the exception of the pulleys and drawlines, there were more pieces of every type than were needed

TINKER TOY MODEL OF WINDMILL AND BOX OF
MATERIALS PROVIDED WITH IT

MERRY-GO-ROUND APPARATUS AND CRATES HOLDING
THE JAR-RUBBER QUOITS

to build any of the models. The object of the Tinker Toy task was to test the subject's persistence in trying to solve a difficult construction problem. (There is a picture of one Tinker Toy model facing page 22.)

Another task was a game of toss with jar-rubber quoits to be thrown onto a merry-go-round consisting of a green wooden disc with four wooden animals mounted on the edge at equal distances. The animals were a goat, a giraffe, a cat, and a cow cut out of three-ply pine with a handsaw and painted in appropriate colors. In the middle of the back of each animal was inserted a metal rod, the target for the jar rubbers. An electric switch moved the disc with its mounted animals at a speed of fifty revolutions a minute. The disc was driven by an induction disc phonograph motor, boxed into a wooden case measuring 22 x 22 x 20 inches and painted a dull red.

The jar rubbers were painted red, white, black, and green, so as to distinguish the throws of the four children under the competitive situation and also to provide a change in color for the three different incentive situations. About two gross of each color were provided.

Orange crates were used as tables to hold the rubber rings and to keep the subjects at a given distance from the merry-go-round. The crates were turned up on end so that the edges, raised about an inch, prevented the rings from sliding off; the open side was placed directly in front of the subject. As many rings as it would hold were piled on top of the crate, and the remainder of those of the same color were put inside, on top of the middle partition and within easy reach of the child. A crate was placed directly opposite each of the sides of the merry-go-round box. Since the heights of the subjects and consequently their nearness to the ring posts varied considerably, each child was first asked to stand behind the crate, which was then moved until he could barely touch the edge of the green disc by standing on tiptoe and reaching over the top of the crate. Weights on the floors of the crates prevented their being pushed forward by the pressure of the child's body. (The merry-go-round apparatus is shown facing page 22.)

This task provided a large-muscle motor skill for a test of persisting behavior. From studying the activity of a few children not in the experimental group, the experimenter concluded that the variable distances would make successes in the ring tossing very infrequent. In the course of the experiment, however, it was discovered that occasionally a considerable amount of success was possible. This unfortunately brought the uncontrolled factor of unequal success into the experiment.

A third task was putting pins into a pegboard with a pair of tweezers. The pegboards were made with hand-drilled holes of a diameter small enough and a bore deep enough to take pins as pegs. Pins with colored glass heads were used for the pegs, the sharp points having been clipped off. To provide a small variation for the three different situations yellow, red, and white heads were used, one color for each trial. The pins were placed in the holes with dull-pointed surgical tweezers. Approximately two hundred pins for each subject were provided. The board was $9\frac{1}{2}$ x 4 x 1 inches in size and was made of a soft wood which was shellacked and then varnished a dark brown. There were fifteen holes in each row for the short side of the board and thirty-seven for the long side. This task was included to test persisting behavior in a small-muscle, finely coordinated skill, with no definite goal. Some of the subjects, however, evidently set a self-appointed goal, since in their conversations they remarked, "I'll do [a certain number] more," or they worked until they had finished one or two whole rows.

Another task was a cancellation game. The subject was given sheets of paper on which small mimeographed figures were sketched in outline. On each sheet there were ten kites, ten rabbits, ten fish, ten leaves, and nineteen dolls. All the dolls, and only the dolls, were to be crossed out. The figures were placed in chance order on the page, except that there were always two dolls in each of the nine full rows. A stack of these pages about three-quarters of an inch high was placed in front of the subject. Large crayons in red, green, and black, were provided for the canceling, one color for each of the three incentive situations. This task was used to provide what appeared to be an automatic, repetitive task.

The fifth task was to drop little round lead balls into a box through a small hole. A yellow cardboard box was placed on end, and a small hole was made in the middle of the top. The hole was just large enough to allow the entrance of small lead fishing-line sinkers about the size of a pea. The closed box prevented the subject from seeing the balls pile up as he dropped them in one by one. Since the noise of the dropping balls might be a pleasant accompaniment to the task, two layers of absorbent cotton were fastened to the bottom of the box with surgeon's plaster. This considerably lessened the accompanying noise, although it did not completely eliminate it. On the outside the box was shut securely against curious eyes by gummed binding paper, which was broken only by the experimenter after the subject had left the room. A supply of balls was provided in a flat, closed cardboard box, with an inch-square opening at one end. It was necessary to cover this box to prevent the subjects from taking a handful of sinkers at a time and thus facilitating the dropping process.

This task was added in an attempt to provide a very dull activity, so that the effects of praise and competition on performance with intrinsically uninteresting material might be estimated. The attempt was not entirely successful, as the median no-incentive performance will indicate. Some subjects showed a fascinated interest in lifting the box "to see how heavy it was getting." This occurred especially often in the competitive situation.

Methods and procedures.—It is obvious that factors just preceding and following a formal experimental period may directly influence the subjects' performances during the experiment. This would be particularly true in an experiment like the present one, in which the duration of the performance was determined by the subject's interest and which he knew he could terminate whenever he wanted to. The schedule of the kindergarten, for instance, varies somewhat from day to day, and the changing conditions there could not be assumed to have no influence on a child's persisting time at a task somewhat artificially imposed by the experimenter.

Efforts were made to minimize these kindergarten influences. Children were invited to go with the experimenter only during the free-play period before the opening of kindergarten, or during the work period which lasted from an hour to an hour and a half after the opening. They were not invited just before the story hour, because in pre-experiment trials it was found that anticipation of the story hour sometimes shortened a performance. No child was taken from the kindergarten unless he showed a readiness to go. His performance was postponed if he was reluctant to go on any day, or if, under the teacher's discipline, he was finishing up a piece of work that he did not enjoy and hence was only too glad to go with the experimenter in order to escape the work. This rule was broken in only one or two cases in which a little coercion was necessary in order to complete the experiment. Subject BA's third Tinker Toy performance had to be forced, for reasons stated in Chapter V.

Even these precautions could not dispose of the fact that what a child was doing or planning to do might influence his behavior more at one time than at another. On the other hand, when a child willingly dropped his work, or when he offered to come just as soon as he had finished what he was doing, there was some assurance that the kindergarten situation was not "pulling" him hard. The experimenter tried further to direct the child's attention away from the activities he had just left by talking with him about something not connected with the kindergarten as she and the child walked across the hall together to the experiment room.

Another of the problems that the experimenter had to meet was the necessity of attempting to equalize the subjects' experience with the material. In each case, before any time count was started she carefully explained the use of the material to the subject and then urged him to attempt a specified performance for practice. Even when the child was familiar with the material from a previous experiment period he was given the practice performance.

When the experimenter introduced the subject to the Tinker Toy, she first turned the handle of the model to show the child how it worked and told him what it was or let him name it himself. Then, after persuading him to want to build one like it, she helped him with the ten pieces that made up the foundation of each model. The experimenter and the subject each made this section of the model. This part of the experiment was not standardized beyond the fact that only ten pieces were put together and no further help was given. The object was to make the child understand the method of putting the structure together. A word of praise was given, whatever incentive situation was to follow, and then the experimenter told the subject that she wanted him to make the toy by himself from that point on.

In the case of the doll-cancellation, the subject had a pile of the mimeographed sheets placed before him and was urged to look over the entire sheet to see all the things drawn there and to find the doll on the top line. The experimenter then crossed out the doll and asked the subject to cross out all the other dolls that he could find on the same page. If he skipped one, the experimenter cautioned him to look hard in order to find them all. The subject was told to put the finished page on the table and to go ahead and finish as many more pages as he wished.

In the pegboard task the experimenter showed the subject how the pegs fitted into the board. She then taught him to handle the tweezers so that he could pick up a pin with them and deposit it in a hole in the board. The experimenter helped him until he was able to get five pins into the holes; then she asked him to take these five pins out and start over again.

In the case of the merry-go-round the subjects took more inspection time than for the other tasks, since the animals and, for some, the motor box were novelties. After the subject had examined the materials he was placed at the correct distance from the rotating disc for his height and told that he was to throw the rubber rings so as to hook the rods on the animals' backs. He knew that it would not count if he hooked the goat's neck or the cat's tail, although it is doubtful whether this procedure was wise, since to the child any success in hooking was probably pleasant, whether it counted or not. The child was given ten rubber rings to use for practice, and the experimenter suggested the best way of holding them; after that procedure the subject was left to perform the task without any further assistance.

The demonstration of dropping the balls into the box, as it worked out, consisted mostly of explaining why the balls didn't make a noise and in answering questions about such details as the paper tape around the bottom. After the subject had dropped five balls into the box, the experimenter instructed him to go ahead by himself.

In an attempt to keep the factors in the experimental situation constant, the same room was used each time and the same experimenter carried on all the research. An easy rapport was always established between the experimenter and the subject before the performance was begun. No child was ever urged to go on with his performance. In fact, before the experimenter left a subject to his task, she ended her remarks with the words: "Remember, you may go whenever you want to, or you may stay as long as you want to." After one minute of lack of attending, dawdling at the task, or extraneous activity, the experimenter asked the subject if he wanted to stop. If he said no, she let him go on. If he then continued this extraneous activity for another minute, the experimenter stopped the performance, and the last sixty seconds were not counted on the record of persisting time. Each child was given only one experimental period in a day, in order to avoid the effect of fatigue on the results and also to prevent the child's stopping one task because he knew from experience that another would be forthcoming as soon as he had finished the first.

THE THREE INCENTIVE SITUATIONS

After the preliminary explanations and practice periods the procedure depended upon the type of incentive situation to be used in any experiment period. In the case of the situation set up to eliminate all incentives except those intrinsic to the material itself, the experimenter explained the material to the subject, instructed him in the specified practice, and then told him that she was going to take her own work behind the screen so they wouldn't bother each other. She then told the subject that he could stop working whenever he wanted to, and that he could work just as long as he wished. He was to tell her when he had finished.

An important source of social motivation seemed to be removed with the experimenter out of sight and ostensibly paying no attention to the subject. There was still a chance, however, that some of the children might be stimulated by the praise they expected to elicit from the experimenter when they had finished and called her to inspect their accomplishment. The experimenter tried to eliminate this possibility by arranging the conditions so that the subject would not have any accomplishment to show. She asked the subject to destroy the evidence of his work before he left it. Before the experimenter went behind the screen the subject was told, for instance, in the case of the Tinker Toy, to take his model apart when he was through working and to put the pieces back into the box. In the case of the merry-go-round he was to take his "ringers" off the posts before he left the room. With the pegboard he was told to take out the pegs he had put into the board. In the doll-cancellation he was to lay his canceled sheets in a box already partly full of sheets canceled in the same color crayon he was using, so that he could not tell where his own work began. The experimenter stopped the watch as soon as the subject began to destroy the evidences of his work. In the ball-dropping the box was always kept sealed until the subject had left the room.

These precautions against a child's expectancy of praise did not entirely obviate attempts to get praise. In a few instances the subject called to the experimenter in a high tone, as though she were in another room, "I've got [so many] done!" or "Come out and see all I've got done!" In the first case the experimenter made no response; in the second, she called back that she was busy with her own work and advised, "You do yours by yourself." Such instances were not usual, but they were an indication that incentives are not easily controlled or limited in any situation.

Since the experimenter gave the same general directions for all the different materials, only one sample for the no-incentive situation is given here. The subject is about to begin the pegboard task:

S looks at materials. E says, "I want to see you put these pins into these holes. We'll put them in with tweezers. You watch me." E takes pin in left hand, clasps it with tweezers, and puts it into the hole. She illustrates with three pins. "Now I want you to do it." E shows S how to hold tweezers and pin. "See how well you can do it. That's right. If you drop any, just leave them on the floor and take more pins from the box. Put in one more pin." S puts in five pins. "Now let's take these out so that you can begin all by yourself. You may stop whenever you want to. When you want to stop, pull all the pins out and put them into the box, and then call me. I'm going to take my work behind the screen as you've seen me do before, so that we won't bother each other. I will stop my work when you have taken the pins out. Be sure to put all the pins in with the tweezers. You may stop whenever you want to, and you may stay as long as you want to." E pushes stop watch as soon as S begins to work.

With the praise incentive the conditions were the same as for the no-incentive situation except for the fact that the experimenter was present and definitely encouraged the subject's activity. She sat at the same table with the subject, at the side to his left. Her record blanks were on a clip-board on her knee so that she would not interfere by diverting the subject from his activity. The stop watch was kept out of sight as much as possible. After the stop watch had been started the experimenter praised the subject for his performance at intervals as nearly one minute apart as his accomplishment made appropriate. An inflexible time interval between statements of praise would be very likely to lead to incongruous psychological situations. Six different phrases were repeated in a conventional round.

For the competitive situation, in which the competition was definitely instigated by the experimenter, four children were taken from the kindergarten at one time and brought to the experiment room. In each of the tasks except the ball-dropping the same four children competed with one another. The personnel of the groups was chosen by chance, except for the four children in the afternoon kindergarten session.

In the case of the Tinker Toy and the cancellation of dolls, the children and the materials for each child were arranged around two small kindergarten tables pushed together. The material for the

pegboards and the ball-dropping took up less space, so that only
one table was used with a child working at each side. The merry-
go-round was arranged so that one child could work on each side
of it, the four orange crates being placed at appropriate distances
for the height of each subject, as described above.

If the group had not had experience with the task at any previous
period, that is, if they came to it first under the competitive situation, the experimenter explained and demonstrated the materials.
In any case, the subjects were given the practice performance. The
experimenter then got the attention of all the children and indicated
a piece of white cardboard on the wall. It was approximately 1 x 4
feet in size, with colored stars pasted on it. (A different color star
was used for each of the five materials.) The stars were pasted in
groups graduated from about twenty-five in the top group to one
at the bottom. Beside each group of stars there was space enough
for a child's name and picture. The experimenter had a picture
of every child in the kindergarten, and she explained that all these
children were going to play the same game that the present group
were playing. The purpose of the pictures, of course, was to make
as real as possible to each group the fact that not only they, but all
the other children in the kindergarten, were to be competitors.

The experimenter then explained that the one of all the children
who worked the longest and the hardest would have his or her
name at the top of the card beside the largest number of stars, but
that the one who stopped first and did the least would have his
or her name at the very bottom. She said that when all the children
had played the games, the card would hang in the kindergarten.
The experimenter continued to explain until all four children appeared to understand. She, of course, stayed in the room, and sometimes interfered if the four children got too excited and started
to use the test materials as implements of war. She was careful,
however, not to praise or to criticize any performance related directly to the task at hand.

The following instructions given for the competitive incentive
will fit any of the materials. The experimenter said:

You have all done this work before, but every other time you did it
alone, working by yourself. This time you're going to work together,
because I want to see who will stay the longest. Everyone in the kindergarten is going to do this. See, here are their pictures. I want to see
who, of all these children, will get the most work done. When everyone
in the kindergarten has had a turn, the one who worked the longest will

have his picture and name here at the top [pointing]; the one who worked next to the longest, here, but the one who stays the shortest time will have his picture 'way down here.

This explanation was then repeated, with the added information that the cardboard with the names and pictures on it would be hung in the kindergarten. The experimenter concluded by saying, "But you may stop whenever you want to, and you may stay as long as you wish. All ready—go!"

It is patent that this incentive is not precisely named—either in this study or in most others—when it is called a competitive incentive. It is impossible in the present setup, for example, to know how much of the increased performance should be attributed to competition, accompanied by the two invariable aspects of recognition by one's peers and by an adult, and how much to mere sociability. In line with Leuba's suggestion for determining the motivating effect of a single incentive when its presence is inevitably bound up with one or two other incentives, two equated groups might solve this problem of determining the effect of competition alone.

Leuba (27) suggests that the effect of reward might be separated from that of the distinction which inevitably accompanies the reward by comparing the output of two groups differing only in that one group was offered a mark of distinction and a reward, while the other group was offered only the mark of distinction.

Presumably this method applied to the present study would entail offering to one of two equated groups the same social competitive situation that appears in this experiment, but offering only the social contacts—with no mention of competition—to the other group. Theoretically subtraction should give the effect of competition alone, but psychologically it probably would not. Competition in the second group would doubtless have sprung up spontaneously, since Greenberg (16) and Leuba (26) indicate spontaneous rivalry in five-year-olds. At any rate, such a comparison was impossible within the limits of the present study. It is just possible that a competitive attitude could be set up in a child working alone, with the experimenter present, by means of much the same technique as that used to arouse competition in the groups of four. Such a procedure would undoubtedly be more successful with older children, however, than with five-year-olds, because some of the younger ones might fail to understand the situation. This type of setup, if successful, would certainly eliminate the effects of sociability. The problem would be to make sure that it did not also eliminate the competitive attitude.

ORDER OF PROCEDURE

Four of the materials and the motivating situations were rotated for each subject so that there were no repetitions of either at successive experiment periods. That is, no child worked at the pegboard two periods in succession, nor was any child praised twice in succession. It was thought that with this arrangement there would be less carry-over from one task or incentive to another. For most of the tasks this assumption seems to have been more or less warranted. It will be seen that the Tinker Toy provided a very instructive exception.

A typical schedule for the four tasks and three incentives was: pegboard–praise, doll-cancellation–no incentive, merry-go-round–competition, Tinker Toy–praise, pegboard–no incentive, doll-cancellation–competition, merry-go-round–praise, Tinker Toy–no incentive, pegboard–competition, doll-cancellation–praise, merry-go-round–no incentive, Tinker Toy–competition. Only four subjects followed exactly this schedule, the four chosen by lot to compete with each other under the competitive situation. Four others started with pegboard–no incentive. The reader may see from the schedule above that this was followed by doll-cancellation–competition, merry-go-round–praise, etc. Each subject in another group was started with doll-cancellation–praise; in another, with Tinker Toy–no incentive; and in the fifth group, with merry-go-round–praise. This type of rotation was introduced in order to eliminate constant errors in group results that might have occurred—and indeterminably—if task and incentive had followed in the same order for the whole group.

The usual interval between experiment periods for each subject was two or three days. In two cases of sickness, unfortunately, this interval had to be lengthened. Each group of four children took approximately one and one-half months to complete its schedule, exclusive of the ball-dropping series. This task was added as a measure of check-up on the other materials. The groups of four competitors in this task were changed in personnel in order to determine whether any significant changes in competitive behavior would result. This task was given to all subjects in the same order, first with praise, second with no incentive, and third with competition.

The persisting time of each child in each incentive situation was recorded in minutes and seconds. The experimenter also recorded the amount of work done and made a shorthand record of the subjects' conversations.

In addition to the experimental setup, questionnaires and ratings were made out by two kindergarten teachers who knew the children well, and another questionnaire was filled out by the experimenter during a visit to each child's home. From these visits the experimenter hoped to get the mother's opinion of her child's habits of persisting. She particularly wanted some account of the influences at home that might have had a bearing upon the development of these habits.

The experimenter also took some time-sampling records of the children's persisting behavior in the kindergarten, to get a possible measure of validity and to obtain a more complete picture of the individual persisting patterns. She abandoned this plan because the results did not seem commensurate with the time necessary to get a sufficient number of records. There were so many unforeseen and uncontrollable interruptions in the kindergarten that the number of time-sampling records necessary for satisfactory reliability would have been very great.

The experimenter is aware that such a procedure as that outlined in this chapter, carried out with only a small number of subjects, has rigorous scientific limitations. The number of variables and the time necessary to collect the results limited the number of subjects with whom the experimenter could work, and this in turn very obviously limited the reliability of the differences, so that the conclusions are restricted to indicating the probable direction of the effects of the various conditions, rather than the probable amount of such effects. There is, however, as we have already stated, a definite advantage in making an intensive study of a small number of subjects. With this method it is possible to get closer to the patterns and inter-relationships of behavior and to discover some of the individual variations which have often been ignored in studies that used more subjects.

IV. ANALYSES OF GROUP RESULTS

The total results for each of the three incentive situations will be given in the first section of this chapter. These will be followed by a more detailed analysis of the tasks as they are related, first, to the incentives, and second, to one another. We shall then examine the relation of the persisting performances to the factors of sex, socio-economic status, age, and intelligence test scores. In the final sections we shall consider the findings from teachers' ratings and home questionnaires.

TABLE 3.—MEAN TIME (IN MINUTES) FOR FIVE TASKS IN EACH
INCENTIVE SITUATION

INCENTIVE SITUATION	MEAN	SIGMAS*
No incentive ($N=99$)	7.2	7.8
Praise incentive ($N=99$)	10.9	11.8
Competition incentive ($N=98$) . .	17.2	13.6

* These sigmas are large because the performances are grouped, for the most part, in 1- to 10-minute periods, which is to be expected; but there are enough scattered cases at 30, 40, and even 50 and 60 minutes to make the measures of dispersion especially large. This condition is unfortunately common in experiments on attending behavior when measures of dispersion are given.

The figures in Table 3 represent the averages of the total performances of the twenty subjects in all five tasks for each of the three incentive situations. Where the number does not equal 100 there were unavoidable absences.

These figures indicate the expected results—that according to group averages incentives improved performances. These subjects persisted on the average 3.7 minutes longer when praised by an adult, and 10 minutes longer in the competitive situation, than when working alone. The competitive situation gave an average performance of 6.3 minutes longer than the praise situation. The critical ratios, moreover, indicate a decided probability that these differences would be in the same direction in similar samplings. For the difference between no incentive and praise the critical ratio is 2.6; between no incentive and competition it is 6.3; between praise and competition, 3.5. This finding is true not only for the total of

34

all the tasks, but also for the separate tasks, for we shall see that
in all but one task this same order prevails: the shortest performance
with no incentive, a longer one with praise, and the longest under
competition. We shall see also that the amount of difference between
these incentive situations was affected, among other things, by the
nature of each task.

DIFFERENTIAL EFFECTS OF THE INCENTIVES

Table 4 presents the median performances of the twenty subjects, together with the quartile deviations and the ranges, in each
of the five tasks, under each incentive situation.

TABLE 4.—MEDIAN TIME (IN MINUTES) FOR PERFORMANCE OF TASKS,
ACCORDING TO THE INCENTIVE SITUATIONS

TASK SITUATION	MEDIAN	QUARTILE DEVIATION	RANGE
Merry-go-round			
No incentive	2.0	2.0	.8–12.5
Praise	8.3	4.2	1.3–45.0
Competition	15.3	12.0	4.0–60.0
Pegboard			
No incentive	4.9	2.2	1.0–19.5
Praise	6.5	2.6	2.3–22.5
Competition	7.5	2.6	1.8–37.0
Doll-cancellation			
No incentive	3.9	2.0	2.3–15.8
Praise	5.5	2.9	1.0–27.0
Competition	11.1	9.1	2.5–37.5
Ball-dropping			
No incentive	3.5	1.6	.7–11.3
Praise	6.6	4.8	1.3–18.5
Competition	11.8	5.0	4.0–39.0
Tinker Toy			
No incentive	15.4	8.6	1.1–40.0
Praise	14.0	10.1	2.5–65.0
Competition	15.0	8.7	3.0–53.0

The important thing that these figures show is the different
relative effects that the same incentive had on various tasks. If
we examine the no-incentive performances in the first four tasks,
we find that the merry-go-round was the least popular. (The Tinker
Toy has been omitted from these discussions because of a special
factor to be considered in a later section.) The merry-go-round
task showed a median of 2 minutes, while cancellation and ball-
dropping gave medians of about 4 minutes, and the pegboard

nearly 5 minutes. Because the small number of cases excludes the use of more exact tests of the significance of differences, we shall examine the amount of overlapping in these no-incentive performances. Of the 59 no-incentive performances (one trial omitted because of illness) on the cancellation, pegboard, and ball-dropping tasks, 51, or 86 per cent, were equal to or greater than the 2-minute median of the merry-go-round. This amount of overlapping is an indication that the 2- and 3-minute median differences between the merry-go-round and the other tasks is probably a real difference.

If we examine the effect of praise upon the median performances of these tasks, we find that the results look quite different. The praise performance of the merry-go-round increased by 6.3 minutes over the no-incentive performance, while with the pegboard, doll-cancellation, and ball-dropping the increase was only 1.6, 1.6, and 3.1 minutes respectively. The amount of overlapping for each of these tasks in the praise over the no-incentive performances is 80 per cent or more in three of the tasks, 65 per cent in the fourth. It is not merely a case of a larger gain for the merry-go-round— which, indeed, might be due to the chance occurrence of a low initial score—but the actual median time score is found to be larger than that of the three other tasks. The amount of overlapping indicates that the relative difference may be a real one. Of the 59 praise performances with the ball-dropping, pegboard, and doll-cancellation tasks only 21, or 36 per cent, were equal to or longer than the 8-minute median of the merry-go-round.

Figure 1 indicates the relative median positions of the four tasks in the incentive situations. The cumulative scores, in addition, show in general the greater frequency of subjects at or near the 8-minute interval in the merry-go-round situation with praise. It is interesting, too, to compare the general structural heights of the merry-go-round curve in the no-incentive and in the praise-incentive situations. These cumulative curves show the variability to be expected with only twenty subjects. It is clear that these figures would be modified by more extensive quantitative analyses. In spite of the variability, however, the curves tend to confirm the tendencies shown by the median scores.

The merry-go-round score appears to have been considerably more affected by the praise incentive than the other three tasks. It is possible, too, that the ball-dropping task, on the basis of the generally higher contour of its cumulative curve in praise over no incentive, was also more affected by praise than the other two tasks,

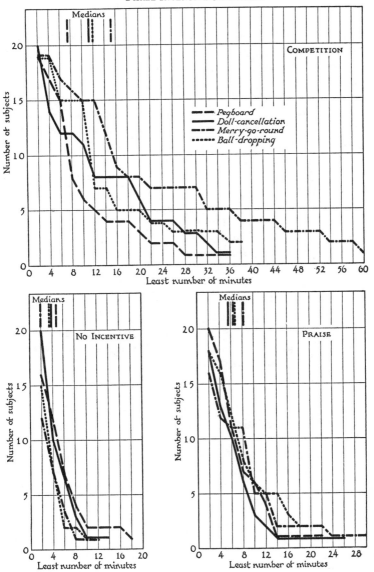

FIGURE 1. — RELATIVE MEDIAN POSITIONS OF THE FOUR TASKS IN THE THREE INCENTIVE SITUATIONS

37

for which the curve contours in these two situations differ very little.

The competitive situation in each of the four tasks shows the same tendency as the total scores for this incentive to affect the persisting times considerably more than praise or no-incentive situations. The amount of overlapping suggests that the differences indicated here are generally reliable in direction. The percentages of overlapping for competition over no incentive in the pegboard, doll-cancellation, ball-dropping, and merry-go-round tasks are 85, 70, 100, and 100 respectively; for competition over praise, in the same task order, they are 70, 60, 80, and 84 per cent.

The four tasks were also differentially affected by competition. Here again, the merry-go-round shows by a generous margin the largest median, as against the smallest under no incentive. The pegboard has now dropped to the lowest place, from the highest under no incentive.* The relative positions of the four tasks according to their median scores in the competitive situation can quickly be read from Figure 1. The evidence that competition had a greater influence upon the merry-go-round task and a smaller influence upon that of the pegboard than upon the other tasks is strengthened by the amount of overlapping indicated. The percentage of overlapping of the total competitive performances in the pegboard, ball-dropping, and doll-cancellation over those in the merry-go-round is 32. That is, only 19 of the 59 performances in the three tasks were equal to or longer than the merry-go-round competitive median of 15.3 minutes. On the other hand, the percentage of overlapping of the competitive performances in the ball-dropping, doll-cancellation, and merry-go-round over those in the pegboard is 74; 43 of the 58 performances were longer than the pegboard competitive median of 7.5 minutes. Individual scores, too, include striking examples of performances on the merry-go-round in the competitive situation. The four highest scores indicate

---

* A comparison of the no-incentive with the incentive performances, in terms of gain, gives the appearance of an inverse relationship between no-incentive median scores for the four tasks and median incentive gains. That is, the order of gains in the incentive situations is exactly the reverse of the order of median scores in the no-incentive situation. Thorndike (43) and Thomson (42), however, show that such a relationship is probably a distortion due to the relation of errors in the initial measurement and in the gain. Thomson's formula to correct for the effect of these errors is designed for use with large numbers of individuals. We shall content ourselves with the conclusion that there is no basis for positing that the tasks showing the lowest no-incentive scores will show the greatest gains in the incentive situations, and vice versa.

performances of 45, 52, 58, and 60 minutes, whereas the highest scores for the pegboard, cancellation, and ball-dropping tasks were from 37 to 39 minutes.

Only with caution should we characterize these tasks as types, since only further experimentation can show within what limits of similarity different tasks can be so categorized. With this in mind, then, we venture to say that the large-muscle motor skill was affected more by both of the social stimuli than the other tasks were. Further differentiation between the tasks was not very clear under the praise incentive, but the children were more sensitive to the competition incentive when working with the repetitive, more or less automatic, tasks than when working with those demanding precision in the use of the small muscles. It is possible that the highly restricted movements required in the pegboard task limited the facilitating effect of the incentives by the strain, and consequent drive for release, put upon the coordinating mechanisms. Perhaps tension rapidly increased until it was stronger than the positive satisfaction to be achieved through the social incentives.

In addition to these four tasks, we must anticipate the discussion of the Tinker Toy. In this task, a difficult construction problem with a definite goal, the group results indicate no difference in length of performance under any of the three incentives. Other factors in the psychological situation appear to have been more significant than the incentives.

As yet we can state no formula for the effect of incentives, except to say that their relative effects depend, among other things, upon the specific task involved. The effectiveness of praise or competition, as they appear in the present study, is apparently an inseparable function of the nature of the task being performed. Even the casual observation made by the mother of one of our subjects hits this point of the experiment. "BE hates to lose in a ball game," she remarked, "but he doesn't mind in a race."

From these data, the point stands out that there are no easy roads to generalizations about incentives. Those experiments in which a single kind of task is presented under varying incentive conditions, with the purpose of discovering the "general" comparative effects of the incentives, are doomed to the limitations of the specific conditions of the experiment. Since Hurlock (22), for example, used an intelligence test containing several kinds of items as the basis for comparing the effects of praise and reproof, she conceivably had a broader base for generalization than had Chase

(7), who compared several success and failure combinations on a single task. Hurlock, nevertheless, can speak with validity about the effects of these incentives only upon an intelligence test, or at best upon schoolwork very similar to the test items. Furthermore, she must restrict the incentive comparisons to group situations, since the tests given were group tests and cannot be generalized to fit individual situations. Chase is limited to making comparative conclusions about her incentives only as they apply to a dynamometer, or at the most to tasks of the dynamometer type. Hartshorne, May, and Maller (17) can state generally the differential effects among their school population of "working for self" and "working for class" on simple addition problems, but they have no basis even for guessing what the result might be for really difficult arithmetic problems, still less for tasks of other kinds, as, for example, motor skills.

These observations are also applicable to Maller's study (29) in which he compared "cooperation for class," with a class reward, with "competition for self," with an individual reward. Maller's is another of the widely known studies that proceed on the assumption that the task is a constant factor in the determination of incentive effects. It is strange that the constancy of the task should be so widely assumed when the Character Education Inquiries have consistently demonstrated a low intercorrelation between different tests of the same behavior trait. If the behavior trait is so largely specific to the test situation, why is it not a natural corollary that the effectiveness of an incentive may be somewhat specific to the task used?

Maller was curiously unaffected, too, by another of his findings, relating also to a factor of specificity, which changed—and challenged—the most general and consistent finding of his very impressive major investigation, although it appeared only as a small, special part of it. I refer to his study of the effect of the nature of the competing group on "competition for self" or "cooperation for group." In the major study the data indicated that the efficiency of work under competition for self was higher than under cooperation for group. But in the special, smaller group, work for an organized team chosen by the children themselves resulted in greater speed even than work for self. In other words, competition for the group was now inducing faster work than competition for self! Maller's task in these studies was simple addition. His results, then, might presumably apply to any simple, efficient habit in a school subject, performed in a group situation. What the effect of the nature of the competing group on the relationship between cooperation for the group and competition for self would be if motor skills or various kinds of manual activities were used is obviously and distinctly an experimental question, and in any generalizations about the incentives imposed the question should be openly recognized.

Before the story of incentives can be written we shall be driven to include in our working hypotheses the fact that the effect of each incentive is relative to the various stimulating conditions of which it is a part, and we cannot assume that a condition is constant except within limits, which "must be proved by experimentally demonstrating that it is *independent* of certain variable conditions, and hence is *universal* to those conditions" (6). Carr's plea for the adoption of a "relativity attitude" was not a new idea. This attitude, however, has been something of a stranger in the study of incentives, so that one would hardly be flogging a dead horse in suggesting with Carr that the psychological quest must be, not to assume constants, but, by "systematically varying all possible conditions," to discover what their influences are. The influence of the task cannot be ignored as one of these varying conditions.

COMPARISON OF FINDINGS WITH THOSE IN OTHER STUDIES

The medians in this study are strikingly shorter than the central tendencies reported in the studies of Palmer (34), Schacter (39), and Cushing (9) described in Chapter II. This is true even when the praise performances rather than the no-incentive performances are used for comparison, although, as we have stated, the experimenters mentioned above set up their studies without any experimentally introduced incentives. Palmer's two automatic tasks, for example, gave medians at the five-year age level of 25.5 and 14.5 minutes. Cushing's averages for her entire age group fell approximately within this same range, while the medians of the automatic tasks in the present study are only 3.5 to 6.6 minutes. In Cushing's data the average for the marble-dropping, a task similar to the ball-dropping in the present study, is 20.1 minutes as against 3.5 minutes in our no-incentive and 6.6 in our praise situations. Indeed, most of Cushing's tasks, although designed to be of a simple, repetitive sort, showed average manipulation times equal to or greater than those of our Tinker Toy task, which has a strong goal-appeal. Shacter's simple and complex tasks, averaging about 8.5 and 11.5 minutes respectively, gave longer mean performances than any of our tasks except the Tinker Toy. The longest performances agreed better than the central tendencies. All of these studies indicate approximately 45 to 60 minutes as the usual upper limit for duration of activity.

The differences noted may be due to sampling, but it is also likely that the variations in experimental setup are responsible. The one-way screen in the present experiment minimized any adult pressure which might otherwise have been felt by the children. We have seen in the previous chapter how difficult it was to be sure that the desire for praise was not a factor in the no-incentive performances, even with the one-way screen. How much more difficult it would be to reduce this voluntarily assumed incentive to a minimum with the experimenter sitting directly by the child! This factor, however, would not account for the fact that our median praise performances are shorter than the central tendencies in other studies. Perhaps the directions given the children were partly responsible. It will be recalled that in the present experiment the children were told at least twice before each trial that they could leave when they wanted to. The other experimenters merely waited for some sign that the child was ready to leave, whereupon they told him that he might stop if he wished. This must have put a premium not only upon the experimenter's insight, but also upon the docility of the child, or, as Cushing has phrased it, his "unwillingness to offend the lady."

The Special Case of the Tinker Toy

An account of the Tinker Toy construction task has been omitted from the foregoing discussions because of a factor that appears to have influenced the results more than the special incentives introduced. This factor was the position of the task in the series of three presentations, regardless of the incentives. An examination of the possible effects of position in the series of presentations was made for each of the tasks except ball-dropping, because it was thought possible that novelty, or the lack of it, or success or failure in one or two previous performances, might influence the following performances on the same task. A test for this possible effect was made by arranging the performance results of each subject for the first, second, and third presentation of each task, regardless of the accompanying incentive situation. The experimenter thought that if the medians of the presentations grew progressively larger or pro-

gressively smaller from first to third, there would be some evidence
that the order of presentation had an effect. The Tinker Toy is an
interesting case of an apparent relation between the order of presentation and the length of performance. It appears, in fact, that this
relation, for reasons to be discussed later, was more important to
the activity span than were the incentive situations.

TABLE 5.—MEDIAN TIME (IN MINUTES) AND NUMBER OF PERFORMANCES FOR
EACH TASK ACCORDING TO INCENTIVE SITUATIONS AND
PRESENTATION POSITIONS [*]

TASK AND PRESENTATION POSITION	MEDIAN	NUMBER OF PERFORMANCES		
		No In- centive	Praise	Competi- tion
Pegboard				
First presentation	5.7	9	3	8
Second presentation	7.1	3	13	4
Third presentation	7.5	8	4	8
Doll-cancellation				
First presentation	5.1	5	11	4
Second presentation	5.1	11	5	4
Third presentation	6.3	4	4	12
Merry-go-round				
First presentation	5.5	8	8	4
Second presentation	10.5	8	4	8
Third presentation	8.3	4	8	7
Tinker Toy				
First presentation	22.5	12	4	4
Second presentation	15.5	4	4	12
Third presentation	9.5	4	12	4

Table 5 shows the medians for each task on the first, second, and
third presentations, including also the number of times each incentive situation fell in any presentation order. All our previous
evidence has shown that praise and competition raised the performance medians over those of no-incentive situations, and it was felt,
therefore, that the number of times any one of these incentives
occurred in any presentation position should be taken into account
in trying to determine the possible effects of presentation order.

Table 5 shows us that for the pegboard the differences in performance time are not marked. (The lower median for the first
presentation may be explained by the fact that there are nine no-
incentive performances in this presentation.) Nor do the medians
for the doll-cancellation show any effect of presentation order. If
there is such an effect for the merry-go-round, it is not constant.

An inspection of the presentation arrays may partly explain the larger second and third medians in this case. In the second presentation the first nine scores range from 1 to 3 minutes, including all the no-incentive scores. Then there is a jump from 3 to 9 minutes between the ninth and tenth ranks, pushing up the scores around the median considerably. The median for the third presentation is larger than for the first, perhaps because there were eight praise and seven competitive performances in the third. As stated in the previous section, if a large majority of praise and competitive situations occurred, we should expect a larger median in that presentation than in one with a majority of no-incentive situations. There is, then, no apparent case for the effect of presentation order in the merry-go-round task, the pegboard, or the doll-cancellation.

The situation looks very different for the Tinker Toy. Here there is a progressive and considerable drop from the first to the third presentations. This is so in spite of the fact that a majority of no-incentive situations are represented in the first presentation, a fact that would be expected to give the lowest, not the highest, median score. Again, in the second presentation a majority of the situations were competitive, a circumstance that would be expected to result in the highest score. In the third presentation the majority represented praise, which would be expected to give, not the lowest score, at it does here, but one intermediate between the other two. Figure 2 pictures the comparison between the presentation-order medians and the medians in the three incentive situations for the Tinker Toy task.

We have already observed that the performance medians for the Tinker Toy were practically the same for all three incentives, a notable exception to the findings for the other tasks. It now seems evident that the cause for this exception is tied up with the cause for the effect of the presentation order. It may be that the experience of failure in connection with this task is significant for the results. In all the other tasks, with the possible exception of the merry-go-round, the performance could be as successful as the subject wished. There was no end to the tasks, since the supply of materials was ample for the greatest "persister" and the subjects were free to set their own goals. With the Tinker Toy, however, the imposed goal was the completion of the windmill, the steam shovel, or the derrick. The fact that these models were purposely made too difficult for completion by any of the children meant that each performance was a failure. And for those who worked really hard and long, the failure was undoubtedly psychologically greater than for those who gave up comparatively soon.

In fact, the position-in-the-series theory very definitely does not apply to several individual cases in which the original attempts were

FIGURE 2. — MEDIAN TIME FOR PERFORMANCES
WITH TINKER TOY IN VARIOUS SITUATIONS

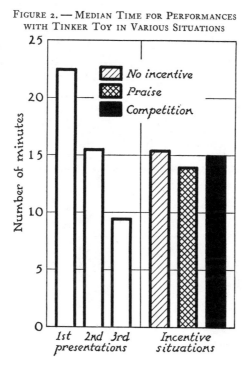

short-lived. For example, subject GD had the following performance scores for the Tinker Toy: first presentation, no incentive, 1.2 minutes; second presentation, competition, 3.2 minutes; third presentation, praise, 5.5 minutes. The incentive order of performance follows GD's usual incentive pattern (see Chapter V). It is clear that there is no cumulative effect of failure in this case. Indeed, there probably was no psychological failure. In no situation did GD try hard and in no situation is there any evidence that she ever intended to finish the model.

There are at least eight other cases in which the effect of failure is not made evident by any noticeable decrease from the first to the

TABLE 6.—SCORES ON TINKER TOY NOT SHOWING PRESENTATION-ORDER EFFECT

SUBJECT	FIRST PRESENTATION			SECOND PRESENTATION		THIRD PRESENTATION	
	Pieces Correctly Placed*	Situation†	Minutes	Situation	Minutes	Situation	Minutes
GD . . .	2	O	1.2	C	3.2	P	5.5
GF	11	O	3.1	C	21.5	P	5.0
BI	15	O	6.5	C	12.5	P	9.6
GC	7	O	11.0	C	6.0	P	11.8
BH	15	O	12.8	C	9.2	P	6.5
BD	22	O	17.0	C	22.0	P	18.5
BF	24	O	20.0	C	12.8	P	32.2
GH	18	P	22.0	O	16.0	C	15.0
GA	26	O	23.0	C	41.0	P	38.5

* The number of pieces is only an approximate indication of the objective success of the activity, since some parts of the task were more difficult than others. This item is included here only for rough comparisons with performances indicated in Table 7.

† Under the heading *Situation* the letter O indicates no incentive, P praise, and C competition.

TABLE 7.—SCORES ON TINKER TOY SHOWING PRESENTATION-ORDER EFFECT

SUBJECT	FIRST PRESENTATION			SECOND PRESENTATION		THIRD PRESENTATION	
	Pieces Correctly Placed	Situation	Minutes	Situation	Minutes	Situation	Minutes
GB	25	O	15.8	C	3.2	P	2.6
BE	25	P	20.0	O	40.0	C	15.0
GG* . . .	20	C	28.5	P	10.3	O	5.0
GK* . . .	22	C	28.5	P	22.8	O	4.3
BC	28	O	30.3	C	19.5	P	8.0
BA	40	O	32.5	C	27.8	P	2.5
GE	17	O	34.3	C	4.0	P	9.5
GI* . . .	19	C	34.5	P	16.0	O	9.0
BB* . . .	28	C	53.3	P	50.0	O	27.0
BG	41	P	60.5	O	15.0	C	15.0
GJ	32	P	65.0	O	11.5	C	14.6

* The presentation order and the incentive order constitute in these cases an ambiguous situation. Although the scores decrease from the first to the third presentation, it is apparent also that they follow the incentive order, competition–praise–no incentive, in which a progressive decrease could be expected.

last presentation. Table 6 gives the raw scores for these eight subjects, and also for GD.

Table 7 gives the scores for the subjects who seem to have indicated the position-in-series effect, that is, whose raw scores show, in general, a decrease—and sometimes a sharp one—from the first to the third performance.

The subjects who showed the effect of position had, almost without exception, longer first-presentation performances than those who did not show such an effect. This is some indication that the former tried harder and probably, therefore, that they had some belief that they could and would complete the model. Where the effect of position appeared to operate, it caused a decrease in activity; that is, no subjects seemed to be spurred on by failure, although the case of GA in Table 6 is ambiguous in this respect, since his presentation order follows the normal incentive order for increased performance.

Objectively considered, subject BI (Table 6), staying only 6.5 minutes and leaving with only fifteen pieces placed, failed to a much greater degree than subject BC (Table 7), who stayed half an hour and correctly placed twenty-eight pieces. But the succeeding performances suggest that the *experience of failure* was much greater for BC than for BI. Although both subjects performed the task in the same order of incentive situations and although in the other tasks BC was at least as much affected by the social incentives as BI, nevertheless BC's performances in the Tinker Toy decreased until his third performance was even slightly less than BI's. (Figure 3 pictures the serial changes for these two subjects.) It seems plausible to assume that a difference in the goals or "levels of aspiration" of the two boys affected their performances, the one suffering much more from a sense of failure than the other. The situation may well be analogous to that in Hoppe's study of success and failure (21). He shows that the experience of these incentives does not vary in intensity with the results of the activity but, among other things, with the individual's "momentary level of aspiration." We have evidence that for some individuals failure practically nullifies the effect of praise or competition in subsequent performances on the same task. This point will be developed further in the individual case studies.

A plausible supplementary explanation for the undifferentiated medians with the Tinker Toy in the incentive situations is that intrinsically interesting tasks are only slightly affected by incentives. The Tinker Toy, for example, was by far the most popular

FIGURE 3. — COMPARATIVE PERFORMANCES OF
BI AND BC WITH THE TINKER TOY IN THE
THREE INCENTIVE SITUATIONS

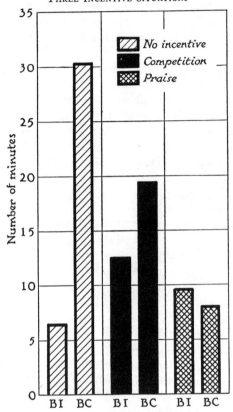

task in the no-incentive situation, with a fifteen-minute median
performance. Perhaps the fact that praise and competition did not
have higher medians is due partly to the intrinsic appeal of the
task itself, which may be unaffected by incentive motivation. The
median scores of the nine subjects whose performances do not indicate a presentation-order effect are not apparently influenced by the
incentives, and so are at least corroborative evidence for this guess.
Their no-incentive median is 12.8 minutes; praise, 11.8 minutes;
and competition, 12.8 minutes. In further experimentation a very
interesting task should be included which does not embody the
factor of a restricted success or failure.

INTER-RELATIONS OF TASKS UNDER VARIOUS INCENTIVES

In this section we shall consider the relations within the group of subjects to determine whether they remain approximately the same from one condition to another, or whether they change with varying conditions. First we shall examine the inter-relations of the subjects' performances in the four tasks in the no-incentive situations. The Tinker Toy is omitted for the obvious reason, explained above, that its position in the presentation series seems to have had more effect on the results than did the incentive situations.

Under similar incentive conditions.—Table 8 gives the correlations of the four tasks with one another when the experimenter was behind the one-way screen, so that there was no incentive other than the task itself.

TABLE 8.—INTER-RHO'S FOR FOUR TASKS IN THE NO-INCENTIVE
SITUATION

	BALL-DROPPING	MERRY-GO-ROUND	PEGBOARD
Doll-cancellation .	+.16	+.41	+.36
Ball-dropping		−.03	+.50
Merry-go-round			−.06
Median rho = +.26			

Apparently there is some correlation in persisting time between one task and another, but that relationship is not close or constant. Since these rho's are determined on the basis of a small number of cases, it is well to add another method of comparing the individual persisting performances. The writer listed the five individuals in the lowest quartiles, no-incentive situation, for pegboard, doll-cancellation, ball-dropping, and merry-go-round. Only one person was on three of the lists, five individuals appeared twice, and seven only once. For the highest quartiles, the consistency is no greater. One individual appeared all four times in the highest quartiles, four twice, and eight only once.

We may conclude tentatively, then, that a child's persisting performance in one task, with no incentive beyond that of the task itself, is a little more likely than not to be duplicated in another task under the same conditions. There is, however, no evidence here that this is more true of the less than of the more persistent, or vice versa.

Table 9 gives the rho's for these four tasks with one another under the praise situation. The rho's are smaller than those for no incentive. An examination of the consistency with which the same subjects remained in the lowest or the highest quartiles reveals practically the same picture as in the no-incentive situation. Two individuals appeared in the lowest quartile in three of the four tasks, four individuals appeared twice, and eight only once. In the highest quartiles, one individual appeared three times, six appeared twice, and five once.

TABLE 9.—INTER-RHO'S FOR FOUR TASKS IN THE PRAISE SITUATION

	BALL-DROPPING	MERRY-GO-ROUND	PEGBOARD
Doll-cancellation .	+.02	+.20	+.26
Ball-dropping		+.28	+.11
Merry-go-round			−.05
Median rho = +.16			

On the basis of the rho's it appears that there is a slight tendency for an individual's performance, i.e., his position in a group, under praise to be somewhat related from one task to another, although the relationships among the tasks are very variable.

The persisting scores in the four tasks under competition cannot properly be treated as the no-incentive and praise-incentive scores were, because the competitive scores are not so comparable with one another as are those made under the more controlled conditions of single performances. The length of an individual's performance must have depended to a considerable extent—and certainly to an unmeasurable extent—upon the persisting times of the particular group of four competitors with which he worked. Rho's between competitive arrays, therefore, are not warranted. Another possible way of estimating consistency of performance is to determine the consistency of the order in which each subject left his competitive group. Is there any indication, for example, that the first subject to leave at one task was first, or second, at another? Again, for how many of the subjects·was competition a strong enough incentive to induce them to stay until after the others had left? The evidence is not clear cut, but there is some indication that there was a degree of consistency from one task to another. (In considering the order of leaving the group the Tinker Toy will be included among the tasks, because the four competing children in any group were working under equal conditions among themselves, whether it was the first, second, or third presentation of the Tinker Toy.)

It will be remembered that each subject (with two exceptions for illness) was in a competitive group five times. Each of these five times he could have been the first, second, third, or last to leave. Of the twenty subjects, fourteen quit three or more times in the same position or order. Only four of these fourteen subjects, however, kept the same position four or five times; the other ten kept it just three times. For fourteen subjects, then, the evidence is slightly greater than chance that competition will affect the persisting performance on different tasks in a similar way. The other six subjects were less consistent, placing in no position more than twice.

It is interesting to see what evidence there is for the presence of a competitive attitude among these children. There seems to be no method by which we can establish a conclusive case for a strong competitive attitude, since the evidence for most subjects is ambiguous. We may, however, put together evidence of two kinds. First, we shall assume that those subjects who were third or fourth to leave in all but one of the five tasks showed fairly reliable evidence of having a competitive attitude. This, however, is not enough, for it is possible that the personnel of the competing group had an effect upon the performance time of the individuals. In a few cases, for example, a subject stayed a long time, and yet left second in the group. To check partially on the effects of the membership of the groups, the personnel of four groups was changed under ball-dropping. However, only one of the sixteen subjects affected showed a distinct change in rank: GF, who in the former group had quit first or second every time, stayed until the very last in the ball-dropping, and actually made thereby the highest competitive rank in the total group for this task. Moreover, this was only the second time in the entire experiment that she went above the median. The writer knows no explanation for this performance. No other subject showed in this task a distinct variation from his former performances. But this was not an adequate check, of course. The influence of the competitors and their personal relations to one another is a complete experimental problem in itself.

It is evident that all the positions, first, second, third, and fourth, are not of equal value. For this reason, in addition to considering the order of leaving the competitive situation, the writer has calculated each subject's total competition score (excluding the Tinker Toy in this case, for obvious reasons), in order to determine those subjects who, although leaving first or second more than once, nevertheless had a long competitive persisting time. This would indicate that if they had been pitted against other individuals, these subjects might have earned third or fourth places several more times than they did.

On the basis of these two types of evidence, only two of the subjects can be said to have shown really strong competitive attitudes. One of these was the fourth to leave every time, and the other stayed until third or fourth every time. Four more stood in third or fourth place all but once. Three others have been added to those whom the experimenter would rank among "high" competitors, because their ranks in the array of total competition scores were very high. It may be said, then, that for nine subjects the competitive situation brought about a noticeable attitude of rivalry.

Some subjects showed evidence of only a very weak competitive attitude. Two of the twenty subjects did not stay beyond second place even once; and six more stayed beyond second place only once. These eight subjects also showed low ranks in the total competition scores. Six of the eight even showed one or two competitive performances that were shorter than their no-incentive performances. It appears, then, that there were eight subjects for whom the competitive situation, as set up here, was not effective in bringing about a definitely competitive attitude.

There is evidence that a competitive attitude is somewhat, although not very greatly, consistent from one task to another. Among the twenty subjects in the present experiment, fewer than half showed evidence of what may be termed a striking rivalry response. The problem of individual differences in rivalry attitudes is important. Greenberg (16) and Leuba (26) were interested in the relation of age to the appearance of this attitude, and found, as we have indicated, that it seems to be present between the fourth and fifth years. The present study indicates that the attitude seems to be present in different degrees of consistency and strength among a group of children of these ages. The conditions associated with these differences in degree can be determined only by a quantitative and systematic variation of many possible associated factors. Several such factors will be discussed in later sections of the present study.

Under different incentive conditions.—In this section we shall consider the relationships among the tasks when they were performed under different incentive situations. First, we shall determine the rho's that show roughly the subjects' relative positions within the group in the performance of each of the four tasks under praise and under no incentive. Table 10 gives this information. It appears from the data that a child's performance is more likely than not to be in somewhat the same relative position under praise as under no incentive, but that the likelihood is not strongly indicated.

TABLE 10.—INTER-RHO'S FOR FOUR TASKS BETWEEN NO-INCENTIVE AND PRAISE SITUATIONS

PRAISE	No Incentive			
	Doll-Cancellation	Ball-Dropping	Merry-Go-Round	Pegboard
Doll-cancellation . .	+.35			
Ball-dropping.		+.41		
Merry-go-round.			+.46	
Pegboard				+.29

Median rho = +.38

TABLE 11.—RANK ORDER OF INDIVIDUAL MEDIAN RANKS FOR PEGBOARD, DOLL-CANCELLATION, MERRY-GO-ROUND, AND BALL-DROPPING

No Incentive		Praise		No Incentive		Praise	
Subject	Rank	Subject	Rank	Subject	Rank	Subject	Rank
First quartile*				Third quartile			
GG . . .	1	GE . . .	1	GH . . .	11	GC . . .	11
GF . . .	2	GF . . .	2	BH . . .	12.5	BF . . .	12
BD . . .	3	GH . . .	3	GE . . .	12.5	BE . . .	13.5
GD . . .	4	BG . . .	4	GA . . .	14	BD . . .	13.5
GB . . .	5.5	BI . . .	5	GC . . .	15	BA . . .	15
BI . . .	5.5	GG . . .	6	Fourth quartile			
Second quartile				BB . . .	16	GB . . .	16.5
BC . . .	7.5	BB . . .	7	BE . . .	17	GK . . .	16.5
BA . . .	7.5	BC . . .	8	BF . . .	18	GI . . .	18
GI . . .	9	GD . . .	9	GK . . .	19	GA . . .	19
BG . . .	10	BH . . .	10	GJ . . .	20	GJ . . .	20

* The first quartile is the lowest.

Let us examine the data in another way, looking this time at the individual quartile ranks under the two incentive situations. The subjects were put in rank order for each task under both situations. The median of the four ranks was then determined for each person, and the subjects were arranged in rank order on that basis. Table 11 presents these rank-order arrays. The fact that the ranks of eight of the subjects (GF, BI, BC, BH, GC, BE, GK, GJ) vary by only one quartile rank or less is further evidence that there is some correlation between a task performed with no incentive and the same task done under the praise situation. It is also significant to note, on the other hand, that eight other subjects changed their ranks by two or three quartiles. BD, BA, GB, and GI jumped 10.5, 7.5, 11.0, and 9.0 rank places respectively from no incentive to praise; while BG, GH, GE, and BB dropped in rank by almost equal differences. It is evident that among five-year-olds the effect of the praise incentive is highly variable in the degree of its influence. We shall later study some of these individuals to get a more complete picture of their whole performances.

Before going on to study the various inter-relationships under the competitive situation, let us briefly compare the three tables of correlation coefficients that we have just studied separately. A comparison of the correlations between the tasks in the praise situation on the one hand (Table 9) and the no-incentive situation on the other (Table 8) shows that all but one of the praise coefficients are considerably lower than the no-incentive ones. The correlations between the praise and the no-incentive situations for the various tasks (Table 10) are more nearly of the magnitude of the no-incentive coefficients, although there is a slightly higher median rho for the former. In other words, these figures suggest a tendency for the task to be more influential in bringing about a closer relationship in performance than the incentive used (praise). It would appear, therefore, that the social contact is a somewhat less stable constituent of the psychological environment than the relation between the child and the task.

Zubin (46) found a quite opposite effect in his study of rivalry. Using children in the sixth, seventh, and eighth grades he studied the effect of individual rivalry upon three performances involving, on the whole, the efficient use of habits already formed: addition, comparison of numbers, and dotting. No-incentive and motivated periods were alternated so that effects of practice were partially eliminated. Under the incentive condition each child was urged to surpass the previous score of the child ranking just above him. Names were not read (as a cautious means of eliminating the uncontrollable and unknown interchild relationships) and the prize offered as a reward for outdoing one's rival was not specified. Zubin found that performance speeds, his measure of the effect of an incentive, correlated more highly with each other in incentive situations than did those in no-incentive situations, and that the latter were higher than those between the incentive and the no-incentive. In other words, performances under similar conditions of motivation gave closer associations than performances under dissimilar conditions of motivation. In the present study, however, the incentive durations correlated lower than the no-incentive, and the correlations among no-incentive performances were lower than those between incentive and no-incentive.

·If we assume that the correlations found in the two studies are approximately in the "true" direction, any one or a combination of the following differences between the setups may have been responsible. Zubin used older children, for whom it is plausible to suppose that, and important to determine whether, incentives have become more stable stimuli than they are for the preschool child. Also, the tasks for the older group were more or less efficient habits, while for the preschool group all the tasks had at least some element of novelty and were largely of a manipulative type. The measure of effectiveness of incentives, too, was speed in one case, duration in the other. Zubin's incentive was rivalry instead of praise; yet it is probable, on the basis of the data as they have been analyzed in the present study, that the competitive situation would not have given appreciably higher intercorrelations than the praise situation. Perhaps more important than any of the other differences was the degree of the subjects' freedom in the two experiments. The younger children were free to leave the situation when they would, while the older subjects were working under a specified time limit and under the conditions of a schoolroom situation, which, by the time the sixth grade is reached, has probably become integrated into a rather rigid, behavior-determining pattern.

We cannot, for reasons already stated, use correlations to indicate relationships between competition and the other two situations. We must resort to making comparisons on the basis of quartile ranks for no-incentive and praise performances, and the order in which each subject left his group, plus his total competition score rank, for competitive performances. A rough measure of the consistency between performances can be made by analyzing the rank positions in no-incentive and praise situations of those whom we have called comparatively "high" and comparatively "low" competitors. For example, we shall try to determine whether or not the comparatively high competitors also earned comparatively high places in no-incentive and praise performances. Tables 12 and 13 give us this

TABLE 12.—ANALYSIS OF NO-INCENTIVE AND PRAISE-INCENTIVE PERFORMANCES
OF "HIGH" COMPETITORS

SUBJECT	SEX	QUARTILE POSITION*		NUMBER OF PERFORMANCES IN FOUR AT OR ABOVE MEDIAN OF GROUP	
		Total No-Incentive Tasks	Total Praise-Incentive Tasks	No-Incentive Situation	Praise-Incentive Situation
GA . . .	f	third	fourth	4 above	4 above
BA . . .	m	second	third	2 above	3 above
BB . . .	m	fourth	second	3 above	2 above
GB . . .	f	first	fourth	0 at or above	3 above
BC . . .	m	second	second	1 at	2 at or above
BD . . .	m	first	third	1 above	3 above
BE . . .	m	fourth	third	4 at or above	3 above
BF . . .	m	fourth	third	4 at or above	2 above
BG . . .	m	second	first	2 above	2 above

* First quartile signifies the shortest performances; fourth quartile, the longest.

TABLE 13.—ANALYSIS OF NO-INCENTIVE AND PRAISE-INCENTIVE PERFORMANCES
OF "LOW" COMPETITORS

SUBJECT	SEX	QUARTILE POSITION		NUMBER OF PERFORMANCES IN FOUR AT OR ABOVE MEDIAN OF GROUP	
		Total No-Incentive Tasks	Total Praise-Incentive Tasks	No-Incentive Situation	Praise-Incentive Situation
GC . . .	f	third	third	4 at or above	2 above
GD . . .	f	first	second	1 above	2 above
GE . . .	f	third	first	3 at or above	1 above
GF . . .	f	first	first	0 at or above	0 at or above
BH . . .	m	third	second	2 above	2 above
BI . . .	m	first	first	1 above	1 above
GG . . .	f	first	second	0 at or above	1 above
GH . . .	f	third	first	2 above	1 above

information. In Table 12 we have listed the subjects whom we have called the high competitors. It is obvious from our previous discussion* that there is no clear consistency in the competitive performances of more than two of these nine subjects, but it is also obvious that these nine children were more highly motivated by competition than the other members of the group. In the first two

* See pages 51–52.

columns are listed their quartile positions in the total no-incentive and the total praise-incentive arrays. In the last two columns a more detailed analysis is made of each subject's rank for the two incentive situations. That is, we have indicated in how many of the four tasks each subject stood at or above the median rank, rather than merely stating his final rank for the total of his four performances. The same analysis is made in Table 13 for those subjects whom we have cited as low competitors. The three subjects not included in Tables 12 and 13 were rated as "intermediate" competitors.

Examination of the tables will show whether or not there seems to be a consistency of performance on the same tasks under different incentives. How did the high and low competitors perform in the no-incentive situation? How did they perform in the praise situation? Five of the nine high competitors are found in the no-incentive situation in the first and second (lower) quartiles, and only four in the third or fourth. By reading the third column in Table 12 we also see that six of these subjects (GA, BA, BB, BE, BF, BG) were at or above the median in at least half of the four tasks. Four of the eight low competitors in the no-incentive situation are in the third quartile and the other four in the first. Furthermore, four showed performances at or above the median at least half the time. On the basis of quartile positions, then, the high competitors show a higher performance in the no-incentive situation than the low competitors do, but the advantage is not marked.

Praise and competition have a closer relationship. The praise incentive placed six of the nine high competitors in the third or fourth quartiles. All nine of them were above the median in at least half the tasks, and five of them were above in more than half. Seven of the eight low competitors were in the two lowest quartiles in the praise-incentive situation, while only three were above the median in even half the tasks, and none in more than half.

It appears that there is a low but positive relationship between persisting performances with different tasks when a child is working alone, and also with different tasks when performed under the incentives of praise and competition. We have seen, particularly from the quartile comparisons, that some individuals are more consistent in this respect than others, a few being generally short-time persisters and a few generally long-time, with relation to the group. Within broad limits, then, we may say that different degrees of persisting behavior, with respect to the time criterion used in the present study, exist among individuals. On the other hand, we have already pointed out the relative specificity that this degree of persisting behavior owes to the nature of the task performed and of the incentive introduced. The chapter on individual case studies will indicate further variables that seem to be associated with aspects of persisting behavior, in both the permanent and the momentary stimulus fields.

Individual Differences and Persisting Time

In this section we shall examine the relation of four factors—sex, socio-economic status, age, and intelligence test scores—to the persisting-time performances of our group of subjects. Since we have found that a no-incentive performance is a quite different thing from a performance motivated by praise or competition, we shall combine, not each subject's total performance for all three incentives, but rather his total performance for each of the incentives. Unfortunately, the method of combining all the tasks performed under one incentive into a single score covers up the task differences. The reason for doing it is the need for a single representative figure. The tables will give us the medians and quartile deviations of the group for each of the incentive situations. Medians for the Tinker Toy will be given for the *total* scores in all incentives combined because the effects of the presentation order are so significant that they have changed the meaning of the incentive scores.

We shall divide into two parts each of the four factors: first, the sex division, which gives a total of nine boys and eleven girls; second, intelligence test scores, in which division is made between scores from 100 to 115 and from 116 to 139, with nine subjects falling in the lower group and eleven in the higher; third, the socio-economic division, which is made between Groups I and II and Groups III, IV, and V, with ten subjects in each division; fourth, the age division, which is made between the subjects from 4 years 9 months to 5 years 5 months, and those from 5 years 6 months to 6 years, with eleven subjects in the younger and nine in the older group. In the division for each or any one of these factors, the other factors were not always equally represented. Since there are too few subjects to make a multiple factor analysis feasible, we shall be able to draw only very tentative conclusions for groups of factors existing together. It will be impossible to estimate the relative influence of the four factors. Preceding each of the following tables, which give the median scores for each of the factors mentioned, there appears an analysis of the number of subjects representing the other factors. For instance, the analysis preceding the sex tables will indicate how many boys and how many girls are in the upper and the lower socio-economic groups, how many in the higher and lower intelligence test score groups, and how many in the younger and older age groups. This will suggest caution in drawing conclusions about the influence of any one factor upon the results.

ANALYSIS

Sex	Socio-Economic Group	Age Group	Test Score Group
Boys	5 from higher group / 4 from lower group	4 from younger group / 5 from older group	2 from lower group / 7 from higher group
Girls	5 from higher group / 6 from lower group	7 from younger group / 4 from older group	7 from lower group / 4 from higher group

TABLE 14.—DIFFERENCES IN SCORES FOR THE TWO SEXES ON FOUR TASKS COMBINED

SEX	NO INCENTIVE Median (Minutes)	NO INCENTIVE Quartile Deviation	PRAISE Median (Minutes)	PRAISE Quartile Deviation	COMPETITION Median (Minutes)	COMPETITION Quartile Deviation
Boys . . .	3.7	1.8	6.2	2.0	16.5	10.9
Girls. . . .	3.5	1.9	6.2	3.7	10.8	4.7
Percentage of girls' scores that overlaps boys' median score	48		50		20	

TABLE 15.—MEDIANS AND QUARTILE DEVIATIONS OF TOTAL TINKER TOY SCORES FOR THE TWO SEXES

SEX	MEDIAN	QUARTILE DEVIATION
Boys	18.5	8.9
Girls	11.8	8.9

Percentage of girls' scores that overlaps boys' median score 33

We shall first consider the relation of sex to the persisting-time performances. Table 14 gives the sex differences for the three incentive situations, with the percentage of overlapping. Table 15 lists the total Tinker Toy scores. The analysis accompanying the two tables shows that the boys have an advantage in the factor of intelligence test scores and possibly in age, too.

We shall use the amount of overlapping as a basis for comparing performances. Let us say arbitrarily that an overlapping of above 65 per cent indicates a tendency to superior performance and one of below 35 per cent to inferior performance. Under the conditions shown for the other three factors, the boys and the girls gave a remarkably similar performance in both no-incentive and praise situations, but the boys' competitive performance is larger, and also considerably more variable, than the girls'. With the Tinker Toy the boys' score is higher again and this time with a relatively less variable record than that of the girls.

In the light of this apparent competitive advantage for the boys, how were the sexes represented among the high and the low competitors? We find from Tables 12 and 13 that seven of the nine highs are boys, and only two of the eight lows, which is a further indication that the boys' apparent superiority under competition may be real. Their advantage in the Tinker Toy does not seem quite so evident. The girls' scores overlap the boys' median score by 33 per cent, and their quartile deviation is very large. In the array for the total Tinker Toy scores, moreover, there are three girls and two boys in the lowest quartile, while the numbers are reversed for the highest quartile. Therefore, the Tinker Toy advantage for the boys is not clear.

In Chapter III an analysis and explanation of the socio-economic status of the subjects was given. There were ten subjects in Groups I and II and ten in Groups III, IV, and V. We shall compare the performances of Groups I and II with those of Groups III, IV, and V. Tables 16 and 17 present the performances for the two socio-economic groups. The analysis accompanying them shows that the sexes are evenly divided between the two groups and that the higher status group has a test score advantage, also a larger number of younger subjects.

Under the conditions of a larger percentage of younger children, an advantage in intelligence test scores, and a fairly equal division of the sexes, the higher occupational group shows a tendency to give somewhat longer performances in the praise situation and in the Tinker Toy scores than does the lower group. That the advantage is not pronounced, however, is corroborated by the rank-order array for the total praise performances; two-thirds of those in the higher quartiles are classified in Groups I and II, while three-fifths of those in the lower quartiles fall into the lower status groups.

The rank orders for the total Tinker Toy scores show the same proportions in the two status groups for the higher and lower quartiles. In spite of the small percentage of overlapping in competition, six, or two-thirds, of those classified as high competitors are from the higher status group; and among the low competitors five-eighths

ANALYSIS

Socio-Economic Group	Age Group	Test Score Group	Sex
Groups I and II	{ 8 from younger group { 2 from older group	8 from higher group 2 from lower group	5 boys 5 girls
Groups III, IV, and V	{ 3 from younger group { 7 from older group	3 from higher group 7 from lower group	6 girls 4 boys

TABLE 16.—DIFFERENCES IN SCORES FOR THE TWO SOCIO-ECONOMIC
GROUPS ON FOUR TASKS COMBINED

Socio-Economic Group	No Incentive Median (Minutes)	No Incentive Quartile Deviation	Praise Median (Minutes)	Praise Quartile Deviation	Competition Median (Minutes)	Competition Quartile Deviation
I and II	3.0	1.7	7.8	2.6	11.8	6.6
III, IV, and V .	4.1	2.3	5.0	3.0	11.2	13.0
Percentage of lower group that overlaps higher	61		31		44	

TABLE 17.—MEDIANS AND QUARTILE DEVIATIONS OF TOTAL TINKER TOY
SCORES FOR THE TWO SOCIO-ECONOMIC GROUPS

Socio-Economic Group	Median	Quartile Deviation
I and II.	16.6	9.4
III, IV, and V.	13.7	8.6
Percentage of lower group that overlaps higher. 37		

are from the lower group. The total no-incentive array shows a fifty-fifty distribution of both status groups above and below the median, and the overlapping shown in Table 16 is not enough to be considered suggestive. We may conclude that there is a slight tendency for the higher occupational group to show somewhat longer performances than the lower in the praise-incentive situation, in the Tinker Toy scores, and possibly in the competition-incentive situation.

The analysis of age differences is made on the basis of a division at the age of five years and five months, which leaves eleven subjects in the lower age group and nine in the upper. Tables 18 and 19 give, for each of the three incentive situations, the median scores for the two age groups in the four tasks combined, and also the percentage of overlapping of the younger subjects by the older ones. The accompanying analysis shows how the two age groups are represented by the other three factors; the difference in sex is not marked, but the younger group has some advantage in the socio-economic status and test score factors.

ANALYSIS

Age Group	Socio-Economic Group	Sex	Test Score Group
Younger group	8 from higher group	7 girls	8 from higher group
	3 from lower group	4 boys	3 from lower group
Older group	2 from higher group	4 girls	3 from higher group
	7 from lower group	5 boys	6 from lower group

TABLE 18.—DIFFERENCES IN SCORES FOR THE TWO AGE GROUPS ON FOUR TASKS COMBINED

AGE GROUP	NO INCENTIVE		PRAISE		COMPETITION	
	Median (Minutes)	Quartile Deviation	Median (Minutes)	Quartile Deviation	Median (Minutes)	Quartile Deviation
Younger group .	3.0	1.6	6.7	3.0	9.5	5.6
Older group . .	5.2	2.3	5.8	3.0	15.0	12.0
Percentage of older group that overlaps younger	66		43		80	

TABLE 19.—MEDIANS AND QUARTILE DEVIATIONS OF TOTAL TINKER TOY SCORES FOR THE TWO AGE GROUPS

AGE GROUP	MEDIAN	QUARTILE DEVIATION
Younger group.	12.8	10.7
Older group	15.0	8.1
Percentage of older group that overlaps younger 70		

The percentage of overlapping of the older group indicates a tendency toward a longer persisting performance in no-incentive, competition-incentive, and total Tinker Toy scores. This tendency, however, is not substantiated by the age distribution among the low and high competitors, or by the quartile rank positions of the older and younger subjects in no-incentive and total Tinker Toy performances. For all three of these situations there is practically a fifty-fifty distribution of both age groups. The advantage shown by the overlapping, therefore, is not corroborated by our other evidence.

The separation for intelligence test groupings was made between scores 115 and 116. There were nine subjects with scores from 100 to 115; eleven with scores from 116 to 139. The analysis preceding Table 20 shows how the two test score groups are represented by the other three factors. The lower test score group has a larger percentage of older children, of girls, and also of those of lower socio-economic status. Tables 20 and 21 give, for each of the three incentive situations, the median scores for the two test score groups in the four tasks combined, and also the percentage of overlapping of the lower test score group over the higher.

The higher test score group, on the basis of overlapping percentages, shows a little longer persisting time in praise, competition, and Tinker Toy scores. There is corroboration for these advantages in the quartile rank positions. Two-thirds of the subjects in the lower praise-incentive quartiles are from the lower test score group, and a very similar proportion in the higher quartiles are in the higher test score group. Among the high competitors there is a large advantage for those scoring high in the test; of the nine highs eight are in the upper group. Of the eight lows only two are in the upper group. In the lower quartiles of the total Tinker Toy performances, seven of the ten subjects are from the lower test score group, while in the higher quartiles eight of the ten are from the higher group.

Under the conditions shown in the four-factor tabulation, there appears to be a tendency for those in the higher test score bracket to show longer persisting times in praise and competitive situations and in the total Tinker Toy scores.

To summarize: It appears that these four factors give no reasonable evidence of affecting differentially the no-incentive, persisting-time performances. The conditions that *are* functions of these dif-

ANALYSIS

Test Score Group	Age Group	Socio-Economic Group	Sex
100–115	6 from older group 3 from younger group	2 from higher group 7 from lower group	2 boys 7 girls
116–139	3 from older group 8 from younger group	8 from higher group 3 from lower group	7 boys 4 girls

TABLE 20.—DIFFERENCES IN SCORES FOR THE TWO INTELLIGENCE TEST SCORE GROUPS ON FOUR TASKS COMBINED

TEST SCORE GROUP	NO INCENTIVE		PRAISE		COMPETITION	
	Median (Minutes)	Quartile Deviation	Median (Minutes)	Quartile Deviation	Median (Minutes)	Quartile Deviation
100–115 . .	3.9	2.1	4.5	3.1	10.5	7.0
116–139 . .	3.3	1.7	6.9	2.9	12.0	6.9
Percentage of lower group that over- laps higher . . .	57		37		35	

TABLE 21.—MEDIANS AND QUARTILE DEVIATIONS OF TOTAL TINKER TOY SCORES FOR THE TWO INTELLIGENCE TEST SCORE GROUPS

TEST SCORE GROUP	MEDIAN	QUARTILE DEVIATION
100–115.	11.8	8.0
116–139.	19.5	10.8
Percentage of lower group that overlaps higher 26		

ferences are undoubtedly multiple, since the differences show wide variations. The activity-span studies reported in Chapter II, which were made in the absence of imposed incentives, show this same lack of relationship between persisting times and age, socio-economic status, and intelligence test scores. The relationship with sex differences in these other studies was ambiguous.

There seem to be two factors that affect the praise-incentive performances, namely, higher socio-economic status and higher intelligence. The higher socio-economic group includes a good proportion of the subjects in the higher intelligence test score group, and the higher intelligence test score group includes a large number from the higher socio-economic group. Undoubtedly these two factors are variously complicated by the numerous other factors that intrude into the experiment, but since they seem to reinforce one another it appears that they are associated with longer praise-incentive performances.

There seem to be three combinations of factors that affect the competition-incentive performance, namely sex, to which is added an intelligence score advantage; intelligence test standing, to which is added a socio-economic and sex advantage (more boys than girls); and probably age. Since the first two factors show both a definite overlapping advantage and an advantage in quartile standing, their relation to competition seems tentatively established. The evidence for the association between age and competition, however, is less convincing, as we have shown above.

The total Tinker Toy scores show some positive relationship with all four of the factors investigated, the sex advantage being in favor of the boys. This task, it will be recalled, was more complex than the others. Schacter (38), too, found a closer relationship between her complex tasks and intelligence than between the simple tasks and intelligence. She had no data for socio-economic status, and she found no age differences in the complex tasks and a slight sex advantage in favor of the girls rather than the boys. It has already been suggested, however, that these differences are not convincing, since Shacter did not examine even the amount of overlapping as a check on the variability of her data. Moreover, our total Tinker Toy scores are complicated by the imposed incentive conditions, which may account for the differences in the results.

RATE OF ACCOMPLISHMENT

In considering the rate of accomplishment, or the output per unit of time spent, only the pegboard, the ball-dropping, and the doll-concellation tasks have been examined. The merry-go-round performances might have included a rather large percentage of accidental successes in some cases, and would be particularly amenable to practice effects. In the case of the Tinker Toy, those subjects staying the longest would be penalized the most by a comparison of actual number of pieces placed. In forty- to sixty-minute performances, for example, the last ten or fifteen minutes were sometimes spent working over some one section of the model, with the addition of perhaps not more than one or two pieces. The number of pieces, moreover, does not indicate the degree of success, since some parts of the model were more difficult than others.

Even for the pegboard and possibly the doll-cancellation tasks, it is not clear that the factor of position in the series did not complicate the results in rate of accomplishment. The number of pegs inserted in the board per minute in different orders and situations were as follows: first presentation, 3.3; second presentation, 5.0; third presentation, 5.1; no incentive, 3.8; praise incentive, 4.8; competition incentive, 4.0. Since the presentation order shows a slight increase in rate, it is not reasonable to attempt to differentiate between the possible effects of practice and those of incentives. We may point out, however, that the second presentation and the praise-incentive rates are practically the same, and that the drop in the competition rate accords with the lower ball-dropping rate in that incentive, indicated below.

The median number of pages canceled per minute in the different orders and situations were: first presentation, 1.1; second presentation, 1.2; third presentation, 1.4; no incentive, 1.1; praise incentive, 1.2; competition incentive, 1.2. The differences in this task are so slight as to give no basis for suggestive comparisons.

The median number of balls dropped per minute in the different orders and situations were: first presentation (also praise incentive), 12.7; second presentation (also no incentive), 15.5; third presentation (also competition incentive), 10.0. Practice should make no difference in the performance of the ball-dropping. The figures for the order of presentation do not show a progressive increase, but drop to the lowest rate in the third presentation. This is also the competitive situation; it will be recalled that all twenty subjects took the ball-dropping task in the same incentive order. It is possible that we have an incentive difference in rate here, with the best rate maintained when the child is alone, the lowest when in the competitive group, and the intermediate with praise. This is further corroborated by the fact that of the nineteen subjects participating, eleven had their highest rates with no incentive, five with praise, and only two with competition (one was equal in praise and no incentive). With the doll-cancellation task, too, in spite of the median competition rate shown, there is some slight evidence that the praise and no-incentive situations induce a higher rate than the competitive.

This evidence appeared from the following analysis of the data: The situation in which each of the subjects made his highest rate was listed. Since there is a slightly higher median rate from the first presentation to the third, those subjects whose highest rate coincided with the third presentation were omitted; there were seven such cases. Of the thirteen left, only two were highest in the competitive situation, four in no incentive, and five in praise. Two were equal in no incentive and praise.

The same analysis was made for the pegboard. In this case thirteen had to be omitted, unfortunately, because their highest performances coincided with their third experience with the material. Of the seven remaining, five were highest in the praise situation, one in the competitive, and one maintained the same rate for all three situations. These data suggest that the no-incentive and praise situations gave the highest rates, while the competition situation gave the lowest. This would naturally be the result of the distractions occurring in the social situation which existed under competition, where diversions were so easily introduced by members of the group. Leuba (26) found, on the other hand, that competition raised the rate of accomplishment among his five-year-olds. He used two instead of four subjects, which would decrease the amount of distraction. It is possible also that practice effects complicated his results.

Home Questionnaires

In an attempt to find factors other than those we have just examined that may be associated with the performance differences, our next step is to turn to the questionnaires filled out by the experimenter in an interview with each child's mother. The questionnaire is given in Appendix II. These questionnaires are limited in their usefulness for group comparisons. Most of the mothers were not able to give very accurate information about the children's play. The prime importance of these visits lies in the experimenter's having obtained information about factors basic to an understanding of the individual's persisting behavior. These factors will be discussed in connection with the individual case studies in Chapter V.

A brief survey will now be given of those items that were differential for the children in the high and the low quartiles of the total no-incentive, praise, and competitive situations. In the praise and no-incentive arrays, the six highest and the six lowest (from Table 11) have been chosen for study.

The lows had in general more siblings than the highs, which might mean that these children played alone less often. Four of the six highs showed an advantage in their parents' education, either one or both parents having been educated beyond the high school, while this was true of only two of the lows. It may be a corollary of this situation that the highs seemed to play with their parents or other adults a little more than the lows. In such play there was more constructive activity and less teasing or mere "rough-housing." The highs were reported less often than the lows as stopping their work to attend to other things. Apparently they stayed by their work at home, as well as in the experiment room, a little better than the lows did. They also showed a little more evidence of helping about the house than the lows did. Five of the highs were reported as having carried on some activity for three or four consecutive hours, while only two lows were said to have done that. It seems that the parents of the children who gave the longer performances had a better understanding of the child's personality as a human being and of the importance of his play.

Very similar differences are found between the six high and the six low total praise performers. Three of the children who were low in the no-incentive group also fell within the low praise group, and two who were high in the no-incentive group were also high in the praise-incentive group. Four of the highs had one or both parents who went beyond the high school, while this condition was true for only one of the lows. The type of play with the parents or other adults seemed to be more constructive among the highs than among the lows. It appears, too, that the highs played more often with older children, and were acquainted with more adults outside of the family and kindergarten, than the lows. They did not so often leave a task to attend to extraneous things, and five of them, as against two of the lows, were reported to have stayed at some task for three or four hours.

We find two rather distinct social differences between the low and the high competitive performers. At least seven of the nine high performers played with older playmates or older brothers and sisters. Among the low competitors, on the other hand, six of the eight played with children younger or of their own age and had brothers and sisters either younger or so much older that there would be no equal play between them; this situation was so reported by the mothers, in fact. The mothers of the lower competitors also reported some "spoiling." Of one, for instance, there is the report, "Adults let him win"; of another, "Older people tease and spoil her"; and again, "Adults give in to her." In our society little girls are probably more likely to be so coddled than little boys, which may be one determining factor accounting for the larger percentage of boys among the high competitors. Among the highs such reports as these were made: "She has to take her own chances when playing with her older sisters"; "He has to compete with the older children on equal terms"; "There is a fifty-fifty winning between the children and their father"; "He plays with his older sister who wants to win as much as he does." These children *learn* to compete from their social experiences.

In the previous section it appeared that an advantage in socio-economic status, in intelligence test score, and for boys rather than girls was in general associated with the competitive attitude. We may now add that this attitude appears to depend further upon social conditioning gained by play on equal terms with older children or adults, and to be retarded by doting and coddling adults and by exclusive play with younger children or those of the same age.

We conclude that the competitive attitude exists, though in different degrees, among five-year-olds, and that, among other factors, mature social contacts help to develop it. This does not, however, imply anything about its desirability or undesirability. Among some children and adults it appears to have become too strong, so that more socially desirable incentives cannot find soil for development. The proper training of the competitive attitude is both a pedagogical and an ethical question, and one of some importance.

Teachers' Opinions

The kindergarten teachers were asked to rate the children according to their kindergarten performances of three different kinds of activities: automatic tasks, problem-solving tasks, and motor skills. Copies of the motor skills rating scale and of the directions given to the teachers appear in Appendix II. There were two purposes for this scale. First, it was to indicate whether or not, in the opinion of teachers, children's persisting performances are consistent from one type of task to another. Second, it was to reinforce the material for the separate case studies by obtaining the teachers' opinions of each child's persisting behavior and the most effective methods of influencing it. It was not possible to get rank-order appraisals, since only one teacher could rank all twenty subjects, while the judgments of two others combined were required to fill out a second set.

The scale used included several factors, each rated on a five-point basis. This scale was not found to be useful as even a rough measure of validity. In addition to the impossibility of getting rank-order appraisals, the range of scores was so small, when the ratings on the four factors were summed for each subject, that the validity of comparing individual ratings with the experimental rank performances was open to question. Moreover, the comparative inconsistency of the experimental performances from one situation to another made it reasonably doubtful as to what experimental performances or combination of them should be used as the comparative experimental scores. This lack of validation is not an important omission, however, because the limitations of rating scales as measures of validity are patent; and, too, an experiment has some degree of intrinsic validity.

TABLE 22.—COEFFICIENTS OF CORRELATION FOR SUBJECTS' PERSISTENCE AT VARIOUS TYPES OF TASKS, AS RATED BY KINDERGARTEN TEACHERS

TYPE OF TASK	CORRELATION OF COMBINED RATINGS	CORRELATION OF FI's RATINGS
Automatic with problem-solving	.80	.72
Automatic with motor skills	.71	.69
Motor skills with problem-solving. . . .	.70	.63

In order to determine the consistency of the children's performances as the teachers saw them, correlations were made between the ratings for the three kinds of activity. A child's rating for motor skills, for example, is considered to be the sum of his ratings on the first four factors on the sheet: attention, staying qualities, ability, originality. Since two people rated each child, the two ratings were averaged and the children put in rank order for each of the three different activities. Since one teacher, FI, knew the children more intimately than the other teachers, the correlations of her ratings alone were also computed. It will be noted from Table 22 that the latter are a little smaller than those from the combined ratings.

It will be seen that, in spite of the fact that the range and variability for each array are small, the rho's between these three activities are surprisingly large. Each set of ratings was collected from a teacher before she was given a second set. Nevertheless, it is obvious from an inspection of each teacher's rating of all the children that she varied individual rating scores very little from one activity to another. In FI's ratings, for example, the median difference in individual ranks between automatic and problem-solving activities is 2.5; the median difference between automatic and motor,

3.5; and between motor and problem-solving, 2.0. These results may be taken either as contrary to the experimental results, which show much lower correlations, or as indicating that teachers' written judgments about children's performances tend to follow the human tendency of categorizing individuals. Although these women are

TABLE 23.—NUMBER OF SUBJECTS FOR WHOM FI REPORTED VARIOUS INCENTIVES AS MOST AND AS LEAST EFFECTIVE

INCENTIVE*	NUMBER MOST EFFECTIVE			NUMBER LEAST EFFECTIVE		
	Motor Activity	Automatic Activity	Problem-Solving	Motor Activity	Automatic Activity	Problem-Solving
Parallel work with adult . .	6	12	8	1	1	1
Parallel work with children.	3	3	0	2	5	3
Teacher's praise.	13	15	19			
Teacher's reproof	2	2	0	11	13	17
Specific suggestions for better product.	3	1	6		2	
Positive urging	6	7	5	1	2	
Humorous corrections . . .	6	3	5	1	1	1
Comparison with child's own previous performance . .	11	11	5			
Comparison with another child's performance . . .	1	1	1	3	1	3
Competition	3	13	7	4	5	9
Insistence upon finishing every product.		2				
Help with plans for work. .	4	2	3			
Group praise	7	6	9		1	1
Group disapproval	2	1	4	8	8	7
Teacher's setting goal for product	4	3	5	1		1

* These incentives are described more fully in the "Supplementary Sheet for Rating Schedule," Appendix II.

good observers and highly trained teachers, it is true that in conversations with them the writer noted a tendency for them to think of the children in terms of typical performances and personality behaviorisms.

In Table 23 we have included an analysis of the number of times each of fifteen types of incentives was reported as "most effective" and as "least effective" in motivating behavior in the kindergarten. These ratings are based entirely upon the judgment of the one teacher, FI, since the others rated the children only on the relative effectiveness of praise and competition. FI's judgments were recorded for each child under item VII of the rating sheet (see Appendix II). The number of incentives listed for each child differed, so that the sums do not total exactly twenty.

It is very clear that, in the opinion of one competent teacher, children vary considerably, even at the kindergarten age, in the type of incentives that will bring out their best work habits. The majority of these incentives show a consistent effect on the various tasks. Praise from the teacher, for example, is very effective in all three tasks, but this is true for more children in the problem-solving task than in the other two. Conversely, reproof from the teacher is ineffective for almost an equal number of children in all tasks. Parallel work with other children, teacher's reproof, specific suggestions for a better product, positive urging, humorous corrections, comparison with another child's performance, help with plans for the work, group disapproval, and the teacher's setting a goal, all are rather consistently low as "most effective" incentives. We should note that these incentives are not rated as *ineffective*, but merely as not "most effective" for more than six or seven children. Parallel work with an adult is effective for many more children than parallel work with children, and more so for automatic tasks than for the other two. This result is probably due to the fact that less distraction occurs with an adult present. Comparison with a child's own previous performance is very effective in motor and automatic activities for slightly over half the children. Far more children are affected by competition in automatic activities—where differences in ability are less varied—than in problem-solving or motor skills. Group praise is very effective for only about half as many children as is adult praise.

The incentives listed are "least effective" for comparatively few children. We find reproof listed the most times, both teacher reproof and group disapproval. The scattered cases are rather interesting. For one child, for example, correction in humorous vein is checked as "least effective." For another the teacher's setting a goal for the product is not effective. These reports are the opinion of only one teacher and undoubtedly represent her assumptions with regard to proper educational practice, as well as her observations of behavior. They are included here merely to suggest that even for five-year-olds the gamut of effective incentives is broad, and that individual differences in reaction to various incentives is already marked at this age.

RELIABILITY OF FINDINGS

In experimental studies of personality behavior, measures of reliability are rare and usually low. In the present experiment an attempt was made to obtain an approximate measure of reliability by having each first performance repeated. The child whose first experience with the experiment was with the pegboard with praise, for example, was presented with that same task situation in his next performance, a day or two later. Such a procedure is open to the difficulty of lack of novelty in the repetition of the task, which only a few days before the subject had performed to the point of satiety, or at least as long as he had wanted to do it. It was felt, however, that a repetition at the beginning of the experiment would be more comparable with the first performance than one at the end of the complete procedure would be.

The reliability coefficient is a rank-difference coefficient based upon eighteen cases. (In two cases it was impossible to get a repeat performance within a few days after the first one.) Its value is .80. The median for the first performances is 6.5 minutes, the quartile deviation 3.6 minutes. The median for the repeat performances is 6.0 minutes, the quartile deviation 3.2 minutes. The median difference in performance times between the first and the repeat trials is 2.2 minutes. The reliability of the present experiment, then, is fairly adequate, when the many factors that could influence a child's voluntary performance time are taken into consideration.

V. INDIVIDUAL CASE STUDIES

Up to this point we have been reporting the results that indicate the directions of *group* behavior under various conditions, as well as some of the possible reasons for high or low performances in any one of the incentive situations. This chapter will deal with *individual* patterns of persisting behavior and with some functional variables that do not appear in the group data.

Naturally, the individual patterns of most of the children follow in general the incentive order for increasing effectiveness that is familiar to us now: working alone, working with praise, working with competition. We shall, however, find at least three striking exceptions to this order. In making a loose classification of the subjects according to the degree of their responses to the incentive situations, we shall see that there appears to be a gradation in the effectiveness of the incentives. Since it has already been indicated that this effectiveness is, among other things, a function of the different tasks, it will be clear that the classification boundaries cannot be sharply defined. The fact that the subjects fit into some sort of classification on the basis of the effectiveness of incentives indicates, however, that there are among the children personality differences that show some degree of constancy and that seem to furnish a variable in the experiment process.

Persisting behavior includes so many processes and interrelationships that it appears to be intrinsically related to the child's whole personality pattern, and consequently to many significant circumstances, both momentary and permanent, that may affect that pattern. In an attempt to discover some of the functionally related factors in the total situation we shall use all the information we have that seems to bear upon the subjects' individual performances, whether they are typical or atypical.

Terms and Concepts

The writer has used various terms to designate behavior determinants, such as *drive, motive, need,* which are associated in the organism with tension systems. For the behavior value of objects she has used *appeal, demand value, interest, valence, goal object;* while *field-force area, stimulus area, environmental field* are used to indicate the total stimulating conditions. She has been loath to use some of these terms, believing that causation and its concepts of force should be ruled out of psychology, so that it becomes a descriptive science dealing with inter-relationships among observed natural processes and operating in terms of events and their necessary conditions. For several reasons, however, she has not ruled out these terms that suggest force. In the first place, since there is no accepted short-form vocabulary to express the point of view of operational description, the phrases that the writer tried to adapt became ponderous and involved; the old words, although many of them were born of faculty psychology, seemed to express the ideas more simply, and there should be no danger to the descriptive point of view if operational definitions are kept in mind. Then too, our knowledge of behavior mechanisms is very often too limited to make possible the use of pure description. And moreover, some of Lewin's concepts have been stimulating to the writer both in studying her individual cases and in presenting them, so that she has felt justified in using a "dynamic" vocabulary until a better one is more universally substituted.

The functional relationships are considered as occurring in an environmental field that includes the positive and the negative needs or behavior determinants of the organism; the factors, physical or attitudinal, within the field to which the organism responds; and the "direction" and "distance" relations of these factors to one another and to the organism.* It has been assumed that all behavior is motivated by some need or needs of the organism, represented by tension systems that are activated in relation to a goal activity and that continue to stimulate behavior until some sort of equilibrium among them results. These tension systems are posited as varying in strength and direction with the progressive and summated effects of the organism's behavior in respect to the goal activity.

The adoption of some doctrine of "inner tensions" seems necessary to an understanding of purposive or goal-seeking behavior that persists in a certain direction despite the single and specific reactions leading to it. Such behavior is readily observed in daily life and has been reported frequently in the literature. Of the several theories offered in explanation of the observed behavior, Lewin's

* See Lewin (28) and Tolman (44) for systematic developments of these concepts.

seems as satisfactory as any, especially since his hypotheses embrace the more complex aspects of behavior. None of the theories provides us with a physiological description of the events. At present, at any rate, it makes little difference to the behavioral principle whether the tensions exist in neurons, in muscles, or in both.

One of our problems is to discover the nature of some of the needs of the organism that direct activity. This we must try to do for the task without incentive as well as for the task with incentive. For neither of these, it is needless to say, shall we find any approach to a physiological basis, but we shall suggest some "second-order" conditions that may be associated with the persisting behavior.

CASE REPORTS

In this chapter only selected cases will be written up in detail. In cases where information pertinent to an understanding of certain behavior is lacking, or where it is very similar to that of other cases, a detailed account would be unwarranted. We wish to make it clear that, although the cases are classified according to a rough approximation of responsiveness to the incentives, some of the individual cases in any group may be described to point up behavior or conditional variables not directly related to the basis of classification. The illustrative points to be made will be stated in each case. The Dramatis Personae appears in Appendix I. It includes each subject's age, intelligence test quotient, length of time in nursery school and kindergarten, parents' education, and father's occupation.

Let us first examine the three cases that present striking exceptions to the usual effectiveness of incentives. The performances of subjects GC and GE were only very slightly affected by the variable incentive situations. Their raw scores appear in Tables 24 and 25, and Figure 4 represents GC's scores.

GC stayed longer only once in the praise situation than in the no-incentive. Although three of her competitive performances were longer than those under no incentive, the totals of all three situations are very similar. In other words, GC seems about as happy to work alone as with an adult or a group of children. The experimenter has been able to find no apparent explanation for this peculiarity in differences in the kindergarten situation preceding or following the experimental trials, but on examining some of the conditions referred to in the questionnaire she found evidence that GC's unusual social responses are related to some of the more permanent social conditions in her psychological environment. Her shy and quiet manner suggested that she was embarrassed in the presence of the experimenter and the group of children, although she had had daily contacts with the children in the kindergarten for nearly five months.

GC's conversation gives a hint of her embarrassment in the experimental situation. She did not say a word to the experimenter, unless spoken to, with the following exceptions, *given in full:* Ball-dropping: "At first I thought these were nails, the tops of 'em [referring to the little lead balls]. . . . Who made the wooden box? Where did you get the box? . . . Guess I am going to stop."—Pegboard: "How are you ever able to get so many pins as this?"—Merry-go-round: "I got one."—Tinker Toy: "I am going to go back." The last two remarks were her total conversation during the competitive performances.

Her mother reported that at home GC had only recently begun to play with other children besides her younger brother. "For years she was so reticent that she cried at parties," her mother said. It may be that an accumulation of unpleasant social contacts partially accounts for this child's lack of response to the two social incentives in the experiment. Concerning competition her mother said that GC showed "about an average competitive spirit." "GC wants to be able to do things as well as other children," she added.

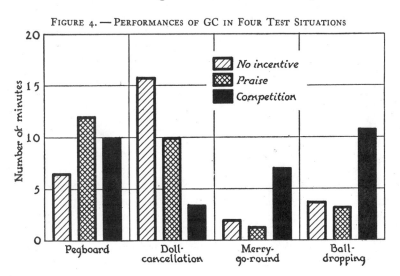

FIGURE 4. — PERFORMANCES OF GC IN FOUR TEST SITUATIONS

TABLE 24.—RAW SCORES OF SUBJECT GC

TASK	NO INCENTIVE		PRAISE		COMPETITION	
	Persisting Time*	Rate†	Persisting Time	Rate	Persisting Time	Rate
Pegboard	6.5		12.0		9.8 (2)‡	
Doll-cancellation. .	15.75	1.9	10.0	2.0	3.25(2.5)	1.5
Merry-go-round . .	2.0		1.25		7.0 (1)	
Ball-dropping . . .	3.9	23.0	3.3	17.4	10.5 (1)	8.6
Total.	28.15		26.55		30.55	

	FIRST PRESENTATION (No Incentive)	SECOND PRESENTATION (Competition)	THIRD PRESENTATION (Praise)
Tinker Toy	11.0	6.0(1)	11.8

* The persisting-time scores are stated in minutes. This applies in Tables 24–43.

† Rate for doll-cancellation indicates the number of pages canceled per minute; for ball-dropping, the number of balls dropped per minute. This applies in Tables 24–43.

‡ Numbers in parentheses indicate the order in which the subject left his competitive group: (1) indicates leaving first; (2), second, etc.; (2.5) means that the subject was one of two children who left simultaneously in second place. This applies in Tables 24–43.

"Indeed, she is so sensitive about this that she doesn't appear in public until she has practiced by herself and has mastered the activity." This factor did not enter into the experiment, because most of the tasks were not difficult, and GC had had experience with all but the simple doll-cancellation before the competitive situation occurred. It seems probable that her retreat from the competitive group was the effect of a long series of group contacts that, for some reason, were not satisfying and resulted in negative or at least very unstable and unsure behavior when she was in a group environment. Perhaps she aspired to more attention than she received. She is very jealous of attention shown her little brother, is very sensitive to criticism, and makes bids for attention at home by "having mean little streaks, spells of expecting everything." Her feelings are easily hurt.

Her desire for attention and her fear of social contacts seem to present a conflict for GC. It appears that in the experiment this fear, initiating negative behavior, was counterbalanced by her positive need for social recognition, leaving her responses to the social tasks about the same as they were in the no-incentive situation. It would be very interesting to watch her future progress, which will depend upon the positive or negative effects of her social experience.

In addition to illustrating the relation of factors in the more permanent environment to the effectiveness of incentive conditions, GC also points up the problem of the specificity of effective incentives. The kindergarten teachers' reports said that for GC competition was on the whole not effective, but that in certain tasks a competitive situation *set up by the children* was quite ef-

TABLE 25.—RAW SCORES OF SUBJECT GE

TASK	No INCENTIVE		PRAISE		COMPETITION	
	Persisting Time	Rate	Persisting Time	Rate	Persisting Time	Rate
Pegboard	7.8		3.0		7.2(2)	
Doll-cancellation. .	3.5	.6	1.75	.6	2.5(2.5)	.4
Merry-go-round . .	1.1		1.75		4.0(2)	
Ball-dropping . . .	3.6	13.4	18.5	10.5	4.0(1)	6.5
Total.	16.0		25.0		17.7	

	FIRST PRESENTATION (No Incentive)	SECOND PRESENTATION (Competition)	THIRD PRESENTATION (Praise)
Tinker Toy.	34.0	4.0(3)	9.5

fective, whereas one set up by the teacher was one of the least effective incentives. It is possible, then, that here the presence of the experimenter in the competitive situation, rather than merely the group of children, was responsible for GC's short performance. While the teachers said that GC desired praise, they qualified the kind of praise. It was "mild praise," "moderate praise," "casual praise" which brought results. More will be made of this point in other case studies.

The case of GE, while indicating a lack of responsiveness to the social stimuli almost greater than that of GC, is nevertheless not instructive from the point of view of any available data that might shed light upon it.

In subject GD we have a case in which praise and praise alone had an incentive effect. In fact, not only was every praise performance higher than every corresponding no-incentive performance, but also four of the five praise performances were higher than the corresponding competitive ones. It will be noticed in

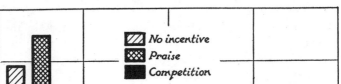

FIGURE 5. — PERFORMANCES OF GD IN FOUR TEST SITUATIONS

Table 26 that the total competition score is no more than equal to the total no-incentive score. The only evidence of a competitive attitude that GD showed in the experiment was when she once asked, "Who's got the prettiest dress on?" looking very pleased as she smoothed out her own dainty little dress. (Figure 5 is a graphic picture of GD's scores in all except the Tinker Toy task.)

We may conclude either that GD did not understand competition, or that she received so much social recognition from continual praise at home that she was not constrained by a "need" to stay at a task that was not agreeable to her. GD is a very pretty

TABLE 26.—RAW SCORES OF SUBJECT GD

TASK	No Incentive		Praise		Competition	
	Persisting Time	Rate	Persisting Time	Rate	Persisting Time	Rate
Pegboard	9.6		12.5		5.3(1)	
Doll-cancellation. .	3.0	1.0	4.5	.7	2.5(1)	.4
Merry-go-round . .	1.1		1.8		4.0(1)	
Ball-dropping . . .	2.5	17.0	7.0	12.0	4.0(2.5)	8.2
Total.	16.2		25.8		15.8	

	First Presentation (No Incentive)	Second Presentation (Competition)	Third Presentation (Praise)
Tinker Toy	1.2	3.0(1.5)	5.5

child, very proud of her appearance, and apparently overpetted and spoiled by her parents and other adults who have lived in her home from time to time. She frequently plays with older children who talk baby talk to her and romp with her. Except in the kindergarten she seems to have no really mature contacts, which may partly account for her not having learned the meaning of a competitive attitude. On the other hand, neither at home nor at school will she work hard at any difficult task. At home, at any rate, she can get praise and undue attention without doing this. It is significant that although in the experimental situation praise was relatively effective, it had no strong motivation; in no instance did it bring about a great gain over the no-incentive performance. In the competitive situation, in order to get recognition for staying longer than others, it would have been necessary for GD to stay at an activity to the point of boredom, or at least to the point of oversatiation with the task itself. Her need for recognition was perhaps not great enough to overcome the negative (or indifferent) valence which the task had for her. It seems to the writer that GD furnishes an example wherein a need is so completely satisfied in certain circumstances that it loses its character of tension when even a slight conflict or negative valence opposes it.

There are four cases in which the effect of praise, as compared with that of the no-incentive situation, is minimal or ambiguous, and the effect of competition moderate or fairly strong. The raw scores for these subjects appear in Tables 27 to 30 inclusive.

Subject BE (Table 27, Figure 6) is dealt with in some detail to illustrate two points: the specific nature of the praise that is effective for his performance and the substitute or compensated satisfaction of a need.

Let us first consider the nature of the praise that affects BE's performance. In all kinds of tasks in the kindergarten, BE was reported as responding to "moderate praise," yet we see that in the experiment praise was noticeably effective over the no-incentive situations only for the merry-go-round. Why was it not more effective in the rest of the experiment? One clue appears in the conversations. BE did not hesitate to talk freely with the children in the competitive situation. With the experimenter alone, however, he spoke very little. For example, in ball-dropping with praise, the extent of his conversation was this: "Where in heck do they go to?" asked as he squinted into the box after the balls,

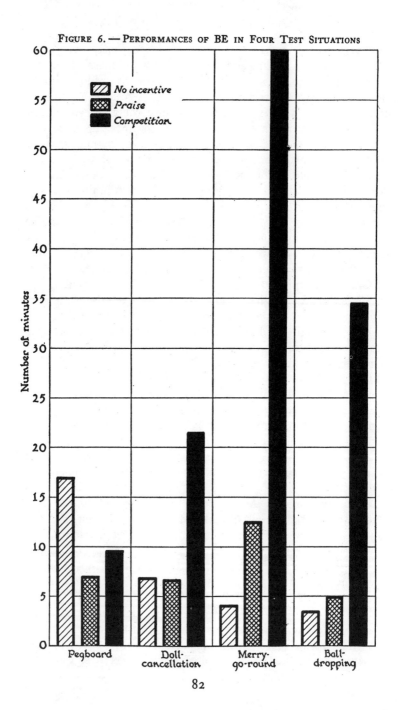

FIGURE 6. — PERFORMANCES OF BE IN FOUR TEST SITUATIONS

TABLE 27.—RAW SCORES OF SUBJECT BE

TASK	No Incentive		Praise		Competition	
	Persisting Time	Rate	Persisting Time	Rate	Persisting Time	Rate
Pegboard	17.0		7.0		9.5 (2)	
Doll-cancellation. .	6.9	1.3	6.7	1.6	21.25(2.5)	1.2
Merry-go-round . .	4.1		12.5		60.0 (4)	
Ball-dropping . . .	3.5	16.0	5.0	15.8	34.5 (2)	15.3
Total.	31.5		31.2		125.25	

	First Presentation (Praise)	Second Presentation (No Incentive)	Third Presentation (Competition)
Tinker Toy	20.0	40.0	15.0(3)

and "Guess I'll stop." There was as little conversation or even less in the other tasks. When the experimenter was praising him, he worked twenty minutes at the Tinker Toy without saying one word. At his next performance with the Tinker Toy he stayed just twice as long, working alone and much harder than before. When the test was finished, the experimenter asked BE whether he liked better to have her stay with him or to take her work behind the screen. "Behind the screen," was the uncomplimentary reply.

The conclusion may be that praise from an adult of slight acquaintance (or perhaps even more specifically, from the experimenter) is little more than indifferent for BE. He always came with the experimenter willingly enough, but probably was not influenced by her opinion of him. It appears that effective praise for this youngster must come from a fairly definite source. In a remark made by his mother there is a hint that praise from his kindergarten teacher might have been more effective. Distressed at BE's lack of neatness, his mother said that she was going to tell him when he came home that his kindergarten teacher (not the experimenter) had called, and had "seen his desk in such a mess." She added that BE liked the teacher so well that she was sure this would work. BE does not play with adults other than his parents, and it is possible that his contacts with them are very limited. On the other hand, he is accustomed to playing often with other children. These social experiences may have influenced the attitudes just described.

Substitute or compensated satisfaction is evident in BE's competitive performances. His competition time scores are very high, but he left second or third in the group most of the time. Only in the merry-go-round did he stay until the last in his group. At this task (his first in the competition situation) he stayed sixty minutes. His nearest competitor stayed fifty-eight minutes, and BE seemed determined to win at this task. In spite of what must have been a wearisome activity, he commented, "I am staying because it is fun. Other children might not stay this long." For once he apparently intended to have his name at the top of the card. At the next competitive performance (doll-cancellation), he and another child left together, second and third, without any particular comment. About a month after the merry-go-round performance, however, as he left second in his group at the pegboard task, he remarked to another child, "I don't care if you get your name at the top. I got mine at the top before." The memory of his successful competition had lasted at least a month.

Examples of this sort of substitute satisfaction of a need—the need for recognition—are not uncommon. Several mothers voluntarily reported, for instance, that in competing with a brother or sister at dressing or eating lunch, the failure to win would be met with such a remark as, "Oh well, I beat you before." BE's mother said she had noticed that BE "doesn't mind losing in a race, but hates to lose in a ball game." Among adults we notice that most of them are sensitive about competing performances only in those games or professional activities in which they have some skill or reputation, or which are considered to be related to their general intelligence. Only occasionally do we find a person for whom the drive to excel is generalized to cover practically all activities in which he engages. This indicates that incentives are never working "in a vacuum" limited by any experimenter's definition of them. It indicates, too, the importance of learning in human behavior and the presence of fundamental functional interrelationships which cannot be adequately described in terms of momentary conditions.

This process of substitution as illustrated here might also be called rationalization. After all, rationalization is effective because we save our self-esteem by means of it. And the desire or need for recognition is—merely in other words—the need for self-esteem. In some cases one has to rationalize lack of recognition because of one's *inability* to qualify. But in other cases one rationalizes merely because of countertensions of ennui or over-satiation. With BE the latter was obviously the case (except perhaps in the Tinker Toy task) because the tasks were so simple that anyone *could* have stayed long enough to win.

Lewin (28, chapter 6) has formulated a stimulating theory of substitute action. In brief it is this: Substitute action springs from or is connected with the tension system that corresponds to the original action, and it must be discharged through that same system if it is to be effective as a substitute. The tension systems must be "fluid enough" so that the two situations, the original and the substitute, are "dynamical parts" in a sufficiently unitary system to discharge the whole system partly or completely if one part is discharged. Since the need to be released in the competitive performances was fundamentally the same in each case, except for the tasks used and therefore the aspiration level aroused, it is not difficult to see that BE might well have satisfied his need for recognition in the merry-go-round performance, and that his winning there might have sufficed for the other competitive situations. He substituted the words or memory of the previous success for success itself in the other instances.

It is possible, on the other hand, that only winning at the merry-go-round could have "stood for" winning in any subsequent tasks for BE. His interest in motor activities is considerable, and possibly he had set a high standard for himself in regard to the merry-go-round performance. Certainly the things in which we excel—in which we set high goals for ourselves—are associated with strong tension systems. Lewin has said, "The substitute value is . . . related to what we have called the level of aspiration" (28, page 185). If, therefore, the need (and hence the tension system) is strong, the effect of having it satisfied must also be strong, and capable of substituting for weaker systems. Only experimentation could tell us whether for BE mere winning at the *first* task, whatever it was, or winning specifically at the merry-go-round, as representing a motor skill, gave the action its strong substitute value.

A further point must be made, however. If BE's standard was high and the consequent tension system was released by the winning that was his goal, then why was not the effect of such success so powerful and, presumably, satisfying that BE would want to repeat the experience? It is plausible, at least, to think that the pleasure might have been so great that he would have wanted to repeat it.

We have already said that perhaps the need for recognition was so well satisfied in the merry-go-round performance that it gave rise only to a weak tension, easily released, in the later competitive performances. Because, however, the effect of success is often to want more success, the writer prefers a more complex explanation, which posits the existence of a conflict of tension systems. The merry-go-round performance was not carried on altogether on the plane of a high goal and a pleasant release when

FIGURE 7. — DIAGRAM OF CONFLICT FOR BE IN TEST SITUATION

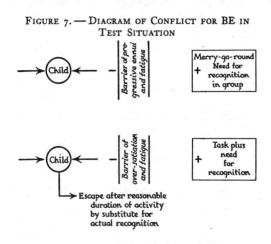

it was reached. We have already said that BE showed signs of weariness, although he insisted that he was having fun. It was obvious to the experimenter that after thirty to thirty-five minutes at the merry-go-round task many of the children were tired. A sixty-minute performance must have been accompanied by real fatigue and by psychological satiation with the task. If this was so, then BE's performance represents the conflict between fatigue and satiation on the one hand and the desire and need for recognition on the other. His behavior indicates that the need for recognition was the stronger impulse, but the fatigue and satiation must nevertheless have left their effect and made it easier for BE to accept a substitute for actual recognition in the other tasks, rather than to buck against the "barrier" left by unpleasant satiation and fatigue. We have tried to represent this hypothetical conflict in the schematic diagram in Figure 7.

With subject BF (Table 28, Figure 8) we notice that the effect of the praise incentive was not consistent, depending primarily

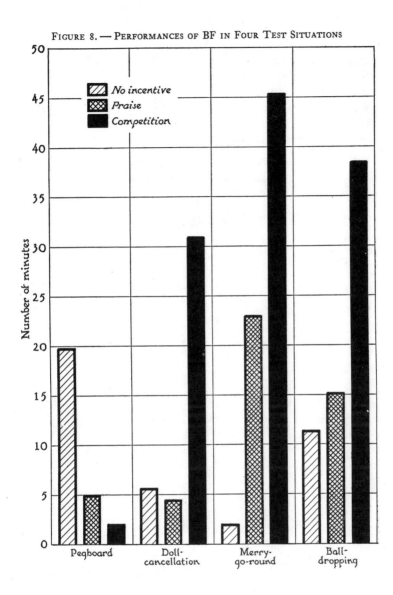

FIGURE 8. — PERFORMANCES OF BF IN FOUR TEST SITUATIONS

perhaps upon the task, perhaps upon factors in either the immediate or the more permanent social milieu. Neither his conversations nor conditions in the kindergarten situation before or after the performances give a clue to the pertinent factors. Our data do not give a basis for any hypothesis concerning the permanent social environment, but they indicate that some explana-

TABLE 28.—RAW SCORES OF SUBJECT BF

TASK	NO INCENTIVE		PRAISE		COMPETITION	
	Persisting Time	Rate	Persisting Time	Rate	Persisting Time	Rate
Pegboard	19.75		5.0		1.75(1)	
Doll-cancellation. .	5.9	2.2	4.8	1.4	31.0 (3)	1.8
Merry-go-round . .	2.0		23.0		45.3 (4)	
Ball-dropping . . .	11.3	10.8	15.5	9.7	38.5 (3)	13.4
Total.	38.95		48.3		116.55	

	FIRST PRESENTATION (No Incentive)	SECOND PRESENTATION (Competition)	THIRD PRESENTATION (Praise)
Tinker Toy	20.0	12.75(2.5)	32.0

tion might be found there. BF's mother works because she and the father are separated, and an aunt takes care of BF and his older sister after school. The family live in crowded, unattractive quarters, and it is probable that BF is not well acquainted with adults outside of those in the kindergarten and his immediate family.

The case of BF is illustrative of the relation of failure or lack of confidence to the effectiveness of a competitive incentive. His response is very similar to that of some other children. The head teacher in the kindergarten indicates, for example, that competition is effective for BF in automatic activities (easy tasks), but that in problem-solving (more difficult tasks) it is likely not to be, because BF "gets fussed and afraid that he can't compete well." Not infrequently she indicates the same thing for other children. Some of her comments are quoted here: "If not succeeding, switches the activity quick as a wink" (of GB). "Competition is ineffective; she goes to pieces" (of GG). "Some competition effective if competitors aren't too far superior" (of BE).

This relation between success and the effectiveness of competition is also shown by BF's record in the experiment. Although his total raw scores in competition show a great advantage in this situation over the other two situations, his separate performances were variable. His low records appear in the Tinker Toy and the pegboard. The conversations in both tasks show that the children had compared how much they had done, and it was evident that BF was not ahead. The mother reports that BF wants tremendously to win. "He even sort of wants to destroy the other fellow's

FIGURE 9. — DIAGRAM OF CONFLICT FOR BF IN
TEST SITUATION

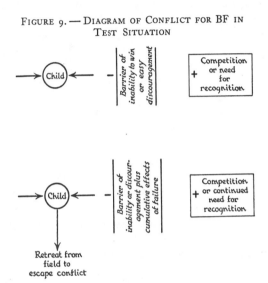

accomplishment, if it is better than his," was her comment. BF has a sister three years older than he with whom he plays often. They compete frequently, and they both want to win. The mother reports that "it bothers BF if his sister beats him." Because the sister is so much older she gives in to him sometimes, but he wants to win most of the time and "gives up easily if the other person is ahead."

This attitude is clearly related to the fact that BF is very sensitive to criticism. He gets discouraged or hurt easily, even to the point of crying. It appears that BF has had some very wounding experiences from failure, perhaps particularly in competitive situations, where his sister is equipped by her superior age to beat him. The data from the kindergarten, the home, and the experiment reinforce each other and indicate that this dominant relationship between BF's desire to win and his ability to win has a broad functional application.

In a competitive situation such as the one in the present experiment, when a child has set a goal for winning and then does not win, the lack of satisfaction or release for his need for recognition may leave a deep effect. His failure becomes a barrier to the continuance of the task. If the child stays in the field where the stimulus for recognition plus the negative stimulus of cumulative failure exists, the conflict is unsolved. Only if he leaves is he no longer affected by such a conflict. (See Figure 9.)

Subject BI (Table 29, upper diagram in Figure 10) had a consistently low persisting performance. He stood in only fifth or sixth rank in no-incentive and praise median totals and among the "lows" in competition. We have no pertinent data to indicate the reason for his relative indifference to praise. Competition was more effective in the automatic skills and the merry-go-round than in the Tinker Toy task, at which he did not stay long in any situation and in which his accomplishment was poor. The teachers in the kindergarten both reported that competition was effective for him in automatic skills, but ineffective in problem-solving, where his ability was poor. It is probable that BI's competitive behavior may be explained on somewhat the same basis as that of BF.

Possibly this child's general low level of persisting behavior may be associated with the adult attitudes toward him at home. His grandmother pets and bribes him, his mother nags, scolds,

TABLE 29.—RAW SCORES OF SUBJECT BI

TASK	No Incentive		Praise		Competition	
	Persisting Time	Rate	Persisting Time	Rate	Persisting Time	Rate
Pegboard	4.8		9.8		2.5(2)	
Doll-cancellation. .	2.8	1.5	2.5	2.0	27.0(2)	1.7
Merry-go-round . .	1.2		3.5		20.8(2)	
Ball-dropping . . .	5.2	16.7	5.0	17.0	11.0(1)	14.0
Total.	14.0		20.8		61.3	

	First Presentation (No Incentive)	Second Presentation (Competition)	Third Presentation (Praise)
Tinker Toy*.	6.5	12.5(2.5)	9.6

* BI's Tinker Toy performances are shown in Figure 3 in contrast to those of BC.

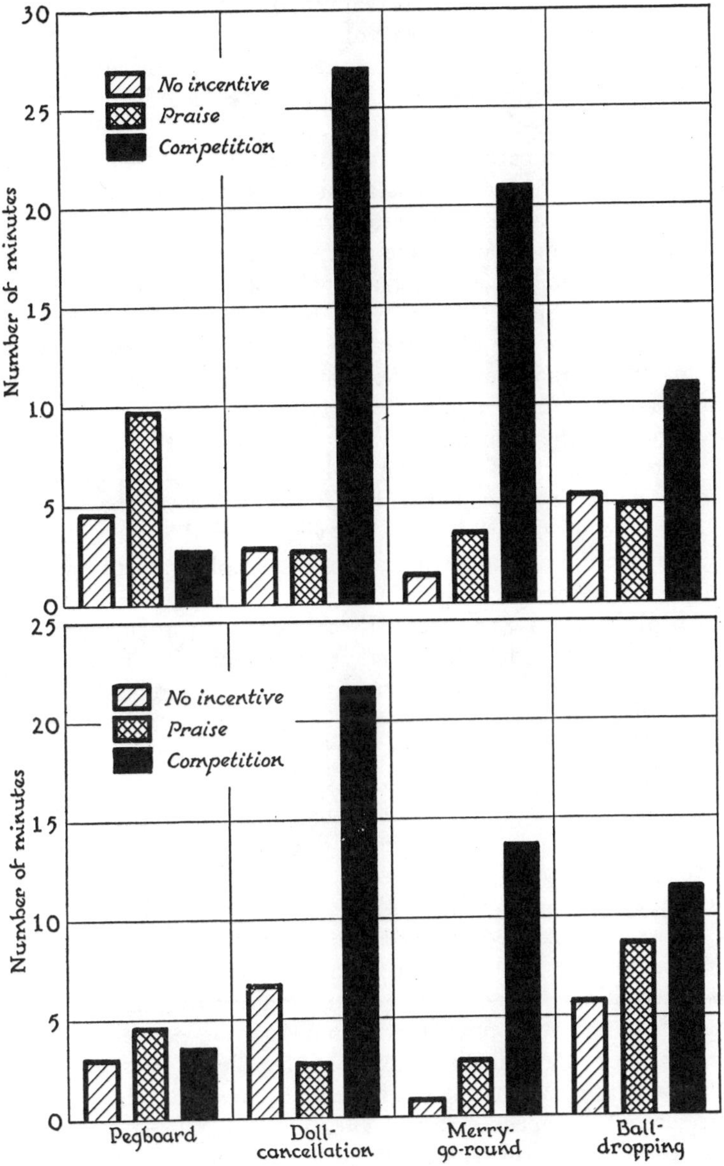

FIGURE 10.—PERFORMANCES OF BI (UPPER) AND GH (LOWER) IN FOUR TEST SITUATIONS

and vents irritability and impatience upon him. The mother's attitude indicated that she expects of BI a higher level of performance than he can give, and this leads to a comparatively permanent conflict situation for him. On the one hand we have the child's natural need for activity of various kinds, possibly reinforced by the sympathetic presence of the grandmother, who not only spoils him but also reads to him and fixes things for him, and perhaps also of his older sister, who reads to him occasionally. On the other hand, the attitude of the mother, who seems to take out her own conflicts on the boy, makes it impossible for BI to get a satisfying effect from many of his activities. The father has been out of work for two years, and the family are living with the maternal grandmother. The mother seemed bitter about the whole situation. She indicated, moreover, that she was entering the period of the menopause, which she felt raised her level of nervousness. She said that she scolded and spanked BI often. "After two or three good spankings," she remarked, "he acts like an angel for a while." In her behavior we find a social barrier (indeed, a physical one in the case of the spankings!) to effective and tension-releasing activity.

It is plausible to guess that BI's comparatively permanent conflict situation has led to a general state of tension in him. Lewin (28, pages 94–96) has demonstrated that restless behavior is one symptom of tension-producing conflict. He has also pointed out that, in children, one form this restless behavior takes is a rapid change of occupation. This hypothesis is useful in attempting to understand BI's low level of persisting behavior, both in the experiment and in the kindergarten. In the case of subject BH (pages 98–100), the same hypothesis seems applicable.

In the case of subject GH (Table 30, lower diagram in Figure 10) praise is not exactly an indifferent incentive—three of her praise performances were longer than with no incentive—but nevertheless three minutes was the largest difference that praise effected over her no-incentive time. In the kindergarten, praise was rated as one of her more effective incentives, but since GH's persisting behavior is rated as low, it is apparent that no method is particularly successful. Indeed, one of the teachers commented that praise is "likely to make GH satisfied with the *status quo* of her performance." It appears that GH's case may be very similar to that of GD, already reported. She too is very pretty and evidently receives so much attention because of her curly-headed, blue-eyed attractiveness that she does not need to court recognition for the things she does or makes. Her mother and father spoil and admire her and buy her the pretty things she loves to wear. It appears that her need for praise is not great enough to make her stay very long at tasks like those in the experiment. Hers is another instance of substitute satisfaction; approval is achieved without effort, so that in effortful situations her need for recognition is not strong enough to lead her to overcome the negative valence of difficulty or satiation.

TABLE 30.—RAW SCORES OF SUBJECT GH

TASK	NO INCENTIVE		PRAISE		COMPETITION	
	Persisting Time	Rate	Persisting Time	Rate	Persisting Time	Rate
Pegboard	3.0		4.5		3.5 (1)	
Doll-cancellation. .	6.6	1.0	2.7	1.5	21.5 (2.5)	1.6
Merry-go-round . .	.9		2.8		13.5 (1)	
Ball-dropping . . .	5.3	13.3	8.8	12.0	11.25(2.5)	8.5
Total.	15.8		18.8		49.75	

	FIRST PRESENTATION (Praise)	SECOND PRESENTATION (No Incentive)	THIRD PRESENTATION (Competition)
Tinker Toy	.22.0	16.0	15.0(3)

At first sight it might seem that GH's competitive performance belies this hypothesis, since her competitive total is about two and a half times larger than that for praise. This advantage, however, is without doubt due to the pleasure of social contacts and is not a competitive attitude. The only remark in the five tasks suggestive of a competitive attitude was made in the Tinker Toy task, when she. said, without any signs of emotion, "Those kids are getting ahead of me." The shorthand reports of her conversations indicate that she was enjoying herself with the group. Her lack of interest in competition is understandable in terms of her very frequent play with children the same age or younger than herself, and with her older sisters, who give in to her in anything that counts with her. We may conclude, then, that she has not yet .learned to need recognition by competition and does not need praise enough to work for it.

The next classification of subjects is based on a moderate re-

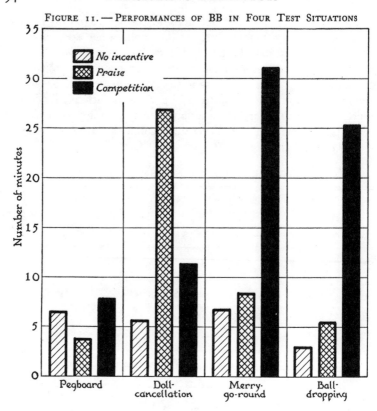

FIGURE 11.—PERFORMANCES OF BB IN FOUR TEST SITUATIONS

sponse to praise and a moderate or more or less strong response to competition. The children included are those whose raw scores are given in Tables 31 to 37 inclusive.

Subject **BB** (Table 31, Figure 11) is included in this group in spite of his comparatively large total score in the praise situation, because that score is dependent primarily upon one performance—in doll-cancellation. In the other tasks with the praise incentive his score was only moderately higher, and in one case it was lower.

BB is interesting for three reasons: first, because of his long and highly accomplished Tinker Toy performances; second, because of his relatively indifferent pegboard performance, regardless of the incentive situation; and third, because of the quality of his performance in his first (praise) doll-cancellation experience.

It is not possible to assign any clear reason for BB's Tinker Toy performance. In the first place, the task was presented to him in the competition–praise–no incentive order, which would lead us to expect a progressive time decrease without the added complications arising from the difficulty of the task; and in the second place, BB was very clever at this problem-solving task, and learned so much at the first and second performances (it should be noted

TABLE 31.—RAW SCORES OF SUBJECT BB

TASK	NO INCENTIVE		PRAISE		COMPETITION	
	Persisting Time	Rate	Persisting Time	Rate	Persisting Time	Rate
Pegboard	6.5		3.75		7.5 (3)	
Doll-cancellation. .	5.5	1.8	27.0	1.2	11.25(3)	2.4
Merry-go-round . .	6.9		8.2		31.2 (4)	
Ball-dropping . . .	3.0	18.0	5.5	17.4	25.5 (3)	12.7
Total.	21.9		44.45		75.45	

	FIRST PRESENTATION (Competition)	SECOND PRESENTATION (Praise)	THIRD PRESENTATION (No Incentive)
Tinker Toy	53.0(4)	50.0	27.0

that he had fifty-three and fifty minutes respectively in which to learn) that his third performance was as successful as the other two had been, although it lasted only half as long. Contrary to some other cases (notably that of BA, pages 109–12) the effect of failing to complete the model was apparently not very great for BB, although he showed clearly that he hoped to finish it. His conversation in the first trial illustrated this. Early in the period he announced: "I think I will make the windmill." Indeed, he both wanted to win and liked the task. "Upsey daisy! I am going to be the first one done. Get my name up to the top, too!" he exclaimed. When he saw that his model was growing he remarked, "I know what I am going to do now. I am going to fix this. I am going to have my name up to the top, I guess. I might and I might not. Suppose I did! Just watch and see if I don't. See if I don't get done with this. I like this." He sang occasionally and talked—more or less to himself—about the work. He finally left without finishing, but he had stayed 18.5 minutes longer than his nearest competitor.

One would guess that his next performance would have been negatively affected by the failure to reach the goal, but in fact he stayed almost as long as he did the first time and brought his model to practically the same degree of completion, this time with almost no conversation. Even the effect of these two failures was not great enough to send him quickly "out of the field" the third time; he worked with as much concentrated effort as before. When he had completed the model, except for an error in the front wheel, he said, "I want to stop now. Anyway, I did the most of it, all except the strings." There is no indication that his failure to reach the goal had left a psychological effect of failure, no evidence of a wounding experience. Indeed, if each Tinker Toy experience was not actually a spur to activity, it was at least progressively favorable to a more efficient succeeding performance.

It is possible that the competition and praise incentives "softened" the effect of the first two failures. We have seen that Fajans (12) found in her experiments that consolation with failure reduced the effect of the failure. It appears to the present writer, moreover, that in cases where failure is a spur rather than a discouragement to further activity the level of self-esteem has not been deeply wounded. BB, for example, knew that his performance was a creditable one; he had worked much longer and had produced a much better model than any of the others in his group. In addition, BB is rated as superior in problem-solving by his kindergarten teacher; undoubtedly his ability in this line has given him a fund of self-confidence or self-esteem that is an adequate substitute for momentary failures.

It is obvious that in order to understand BB's case one must consider factors in a broad environmental field. His pegboard performance is merely an illustration of the importance of the task for the effectiveness of the incentives. He simply did not need the recognition enough to continue at a task which had a very slight appeal for him even when it was accompanied by competition. Moreover, the pegboard task came in BB's third competitive experience, after he had made high competitive records in other tasks, which probably served as a substitute in this case where the task had an indifferent demand value or quickly became negative for him.

BB's long doll-cancellation performance under praise was very unusual. It was his first performance in the experiment, as well as his first with this particular task, and for some reason he stayed

FIGURE 12.—DOLL-CANCELLATION SHEET CANCELED BY BB

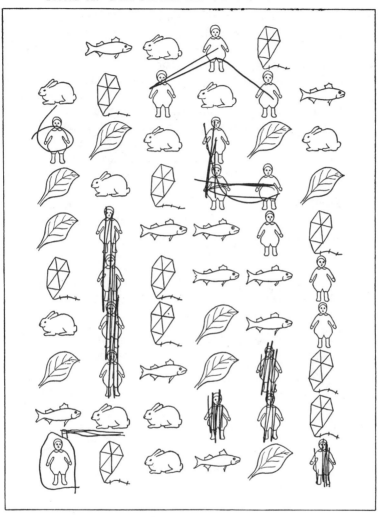

on and on, although his activities indicated that he probably was getting satiated with the task. There is no way to discover the reason for this long performance, but it is interesting to observe the progressive change in pattern or quality of his attack. He started by following a pattern very similar to that given by the experimenter—single lines through each doll, or occasionally a line through two dolls in juxtaposition. Then he began to take in two, three, or four dolls with each stroke. After this he began to slide his crayon over the page, lifting it only once or twice and hitting the dolls with a sweep. Finally he combined this last method with one in which he rubbed out whole figures with many lines, and in a few instances drew a crude house around one of the dolls. (See Figure 12.) In these ways he varied his performance so that he was able to carry on without an overburdening satiation. He knew that he could stop when he wanted to. The question is this: Did he develop the variable methods so that he could stay to reach a self-imposed goal, or did the possibilities of variation make the task appealing? His later performances were shorter; the further possibilities of variation were at a minimum, and by this time satiation came relatively quickly.

TABLE 32.—RAW SCORES OF SUBJECT BH

TASK	NO INCENTIVE		PRAISE		COMPETITION	
	Persisting Time	Rate	Persisting Time	Rate	Persisting Time	Rate
Pegboard	3.8		6.8		6.2 (4)	
Doll-cancellation. .	2.5	1.2	1.0	1.0	18.75(1)	.6
Merry-go-round . .	5.6		8.3		16.5 (1)	
Ball-dropping . . .	4.1	11.0	6.0	12.7	15.25(2.5)	7.0
Total.	16.0		22.1		56.7	

	FIRST PRESENTATION (No Incentive)	SECOND PRESENTATION (Competition)	THIRD PRESENTATION (Praise)
Tinker Toy	12.75	9.0(1)	6.5

Although subject BH (Table 32) showed a moderate response to praise and a fairly high total competition score, the quality of his persisting behavior was poor in almost every instance. He was very readily diverted to things, actions, and conversation irrelevant to the task in hand, and, too, his relatively high competitive performance was primarily due to a social incentive rather than a competitive one. In the group he watched the other children, worked spasmodically, talked and giggled, made silly noises and other bids for attention.

BH's response to certain incentives is something of an enigma. One teacher reports that too much praise makes BH stop trying. In fact, he is one of the two children for whom adult reproof and disapproval were rated as among the most effective incentives. At home his mother reports that he usually does not want praise unless he asks for it, and that he expresses disgust when "people lay it on thick," as he puts it. BH is an intelligent child and perfectly capable of seeing that he is not competent in most activities. Is it possible that he can detect that praise "laid on thick" is not congruous with his activities? Or is it possible that most of the praise he gets is unpleasantly tinged with the hint that he might always perform at that level instead of in his usual slipshod way? We shall see that he has received enough nagging criticism at home to have *learned* to want to avoid it, perhaps thus making it an effective incentive. But the reason why praise—even lavish praise —should fail to bring about a satisfactory performance is not readily determined.

BH's level of persisting is so uneven that it seems instructive to look for contributing factors in his more or less permanent milieu. In the first place, BH is unfortunately very large for his age, so that too much has always been expected of him. This fact gives a plausible basis for the lack of confidence evident in his attempts to get attention by silly behavior and negativisms and in his unwillingness to stick at a task long enough to try himself out. Besides this there is evidence that some of his difficulty lies in jealousy of his two-year-old brother, which the mother fosters by her frank admiration of the baby. For example, she told the experimenter, "BH is just like myself—irritable and unwilling to stick to what he doesn't like," and then openly made a comparison in favor of KH, the baby: "KH is different. He is like his father." BH's awareness of this comparison shows in his plaguing and teasing KH frequently and wanting to do whatever the little child is doing.

BH comes from a home with many advantages, and his father shows an interest in sharing some activities with the boy. His mother is very much worried about BH's instability. Obviously her attitude toward him—of irritability, worry, criticism, unfavorable comparison with the little brother, and frequent scolding—is not conducive to a satisfying work or play atmosphere for BH. His erratic, quickly changing behavior is clearly a symptom of a general state of tension based upon fundamental conflict. His need for free and satisfying activity meets the barrier of too high expectations for him and too obvious approval for his baby brother, with the consequent negative effects from which he cannot escape while in his home. We see the results of this conflict in his restless behavior, which is symptomatic of his quest for a release of the tension systems.

TABLE 33.—RAW SCORES OF SUBJECT GG

TASK	NO INCENTIVE		PRAISE		COMPETITION	
	Persisting Time	Rate	Persisting Time	Rate	Persisting Time	Rate
Pegboard	4.7		5.5		7.5(3)	
Doll-cancellation. .	2.8	1.0	6.2	1.0	8.8(1)	1.2
Merry-go-round . .	1.0		4.1		12.0(1)	
Ball-dropping . . .	.6	14.0	1.3	23.0	11.8(1)	10.2
Total.	9.1		17.1		40.1	

	FIRST PRESENTATION (Competition)	SECOND PRESENTATION (Praise)	THIRD PRESENTATION (No Incentive)
Tinker Toy	28.5(1.5)	10.25	5.0

GG (Table 33) is an example of a child with a very weak need for manipulation or goal-seeking. Her interests lie largely in romping and doing stunts. She seems to have very little need for recognition of the type provided in the experiment. At home little is expected of her, and she is pampered, petted, and sheltered by all the adults (parents and relatives) with whom she comes in contact daily. Praise and approval are too easily gained to induce her to expend effort to get them.

GF (Table 34) has a record much like that of GG with an amazing exception in the ball-dropping with competition. In this task situation she stayed until the last in her group and made the highest competition score in the whole experimental group in this task. We have no data that throw light on the reason for this performance except that the child's mother said she and the grandmother were trying very hard to impress upon GF that she must try to excel other children. GF seemed to be in a transition stage with regard to the competitive attitude.

BC (Table 35) showed a strong competitive attitude for the first and second competitive situations, in the pegboard and Tinker

TABLE 34.—RAW SCORES OF SUBJECT GF

TASK	No Incentive		Praise		Competition	
	Persisting Time	Rate	Persisting Time	Rate	Persisting Time	Rate
Pegboard	1.25		2.25		7.5 (1)	
Doll-cancellation. .	2.3	1.7	2.0	1.5	3.25(2.5)	1.2
Merry-go-round . .	1.5		3.1		15.0 (2)	
Ball-dropping . . .	2.6	16.1	3.5	20.8	39.0 (4)	11.4
Total.	7.65		10.85		64.75	

	First Presentation (No Incentive)	Second Presentation (Competition)	Third Presentation (Praise)
Tinker Toy	3.0	21.5(2)	5.0

TABLE 35.—RAW SCORES OF SUBJECT BC

TASK	No Incentive		Praise		Competition	
	Persisting Time	Rate	Persisting Time	Rate	Persisting Time	Rate
Pegboard	1.2		7.5		19.5(3)	
Doll-cancellation. .	3.0	1.0	5.0	1.0	2.5(2.5)	.8
Merry-go-round . .	2.0		1.9		9.5(3)	
Ball-dropping . . .	3.0	11.0	6.0	12.3	4.0(3)	10.0
Total.	9.2		20.4		35.5	

	First Presentation (No Incentive)	Second Presentation (Competition)	Third Presentation (Praise)
Tinker Toy	30.3	19.5(4)	8.0

Toy tasks, but it weakened in the later ones. Perhaps his need for recognition in this situation was already partially met by some development of substitute satisfaction. His case is similar to that of BE, already detailed.

In the section on the special case of the Tinker Toy we have already seen illustrations of the cumulative effect of failure. Subject BG (Table 36) appears to be a representative case. After his first long Tinker Toy performance of an hour, he did not try to make either of the other models nearly so complete as he had the first one. BG is also an example of a child who seems to re-

TABLE 36.—RAW SCORES OF SUBJECT BG

TASK	No Incentive		Praise		Competition	
	Persisting Time	Rate	Persisting Time	Rate	Persisting Time	Rate
Pegboard	2.6		5.0		10.5 (3)	
Doll-cancellation. .	9.0	.9	3.0	1.7	31.5 (4)	1.0
Merry-go-round . .	5.3		9.0		52.0 (2)	
Ball-dropping . . .	.9	15.0	3.0	14.0	11.25(2.5)	12.0
Total.	17.8		20.0		105.25	

	FIRST PRESENTATION (Praise)	SECOND PRESENTATION (No Incentive)	THIRD PRESENTATION (Competition)
Tinker Toy	60.5	15.0	15.0(3)

TABLE 37.—RAW SCORES OF SUBJECT GK

TASK	No Incentive		Praise		Competition	
	Persisting Time	Rate	Persisting Time	Rate	Persisting Time	Rate
Pegboard	8.0		10.75		7.4 (1)	
Doll-cancellation. .	7.0	.9	8.3	1.2	11.2 (3)	1.3
Merry-go-round . .	5.5		2.5		30.25(3)	
Ball-dropping . . .	8.0	11.0	9.0	11.0	11.3 (1)	8.3
Total.	28.5		30.55		60.15	

	FIRST PRESENTATION (Competition)	SECOND PRESENTATION (Praise)	THIRD PRESENTATION (No Incentive)
Tinker Toy	28.5(1.5)	22.8	4.25

quire a specific kind of praise for the greatest effectiveness. As reported by the kindergarten teacher, the proper kind for BG is *"casual* praise by an adult."

With regard to the incentive performances of both BG and GK (Table 37) we have no striking data that add validity to our previous hypotheses. We may suppose, however, that BG's higher competitive scores have a basis in training at home, where he competes with his father and little brother and is required to "take his beatings." GK's mother was unable to report on the child's competitive attitude, except to say that she was pouty if she did not win when the children competed to see who could dress the fastest. In the experiment, although competition was an effective incentive, GK did not show a need strong enough to induce her in a majority of instances to stay beyond first or second place in her group.

The last grouping of cases consists of those children for whom the effect of both praise and competition was considerable. Tables 38 to 43 give their raw scores.

TABLE 38.—RAW SCORES OF SUBJECT GA

TASK	No Incentive		Praise		Competition	
	Persisting Time	Rate	Persisting Time	Rate	Persisting Time	Rate
Pegboard	5.0		10.0		37.0 (4)	
Doll-cancellation	4.2	1.7	12.75	1.9	5.25(4)	1.7
Merry-go-round	3.0		8.8		15.25(3)*	
Ball-dropping	5.7	18.2	18.5	14.7	20.5 (4)	11.2
Total	17.9		50.05		78.0	

	First Presentation (No Incentive)	Second Presentation (Competition)	Third Presentation (Praise)
Tinker Toy	23.0	41.0(4)	38.5

* Since one child in the group was absent, GA was the last to leave in this task too.

Subject GA (Table 38, Figure 13) is a conspicuous example of a consistently long performer in all the situations in the experiment. She ranked fourteenth in no-incentive medians, nineteenth in praise, and was the most consistent "high" competitor in the entire group. The *degree* of the incentive effects for GA was different for the various tasks; but the consistent *direction* of increasing duration from no-incentive to praise to competition indicates that these social incentives had a general or constant positive valence, within the limits of the experiment. That is, the incentives always had an effect in the expected direction, except in doll-cancellation, where the competitive score was smaller than the praise score. Even in this case GA stayed two minutes longer than

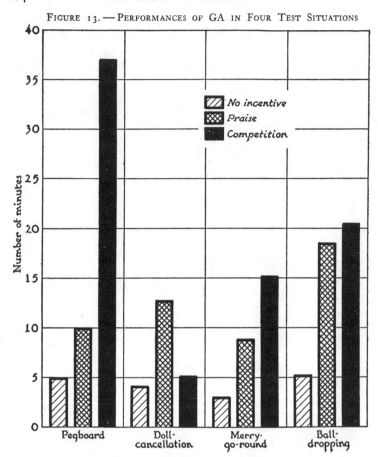

FIGURE 13. — PERFORMANCES OF GA IN FOUR TEST SITUATIONS

her nearest competitor. Her competitive scores are more impressive than the raw scores would indicate; she is the only subject in the entire group who stayed every time until the last in her competing group. In the pegboard she stayed eleven minutes longer than her nearest competitor; in doll-cancellation, two minutes longer; in ball-dropping, five minutes longer; and in the Tinker Toy, nineteen minutes longer.

Undoubtedly the limits within which these incentives are constant for GA would appear under the variable conditions of high degrees of psychological failure, oversatiation, fatigue, and competitors equally determined to win. Indeed, one teacher in the kindergarten wrote of GA's response to competition, "If doubtful about her ability, she washes her hands of the affair. At other times, she goes pell-mell into it to make it best."

Under the experimental conditions, however, GA was easily able to surpass her competitors, and in the Tinker Toy her psychological failure was evidently not very strong, because in no case did she indicate a driving purpose to finish the model. Indeed, her Tinker Toy performance follows the incentive order rather than a decreasing-with-presentation order (which is in decided contrast to the case of BA, pages 109–12). There was a sign of a slight conflict at the third presentation which does not show up in the time record. It appears that the task had lost some appeal for her because of its difficulty, for she remarked as she entered the room. "Oh-oh, there's that game again. I'm glad I'm not you, because you have to do all that!" pointing to the model. The praise which accompanied this third presentation was clearly a factor in keeping her at the task, for very frequently she looked up expectantly for the approval of the experimenter, and she relieved the tedium of the performance by talking as she worked about topics on the radio and in the movies. The positive valence the task held because of its relation to satisfying her desire for praise was apparently stronger than the negative valence it held because of its difficulty. The conflict was therefore easily resolved in the direction of the task, at least for a comparatively long time.

GA's high level of performance throughout all the conditions is associated with a home where her contacts are mature and understanding, where her superior ability is recognized by general approval, and where she plays competitively with older sisters and playmates. This implies no necessary relationships between these factors, but does corroborate other evidence that environmental conditions are functional in varying persisting behavior.

Subjects BD and GI, twin brother and sister, are interesting from the point of view of qualitative differences in their performances. Although both were highly responsive to the social stimuli in the experiment, and although their raw scores are fairly similar, yet the pictures of their performances vary widely. Their raw scores appear in Tables 39 and 40; their bar diagrams in Figure 14. GI's performances were all more quiet than BD's; they showed less extraneous activity and gave a higher rate of accomplishment. These differences were more marked in the social situations than

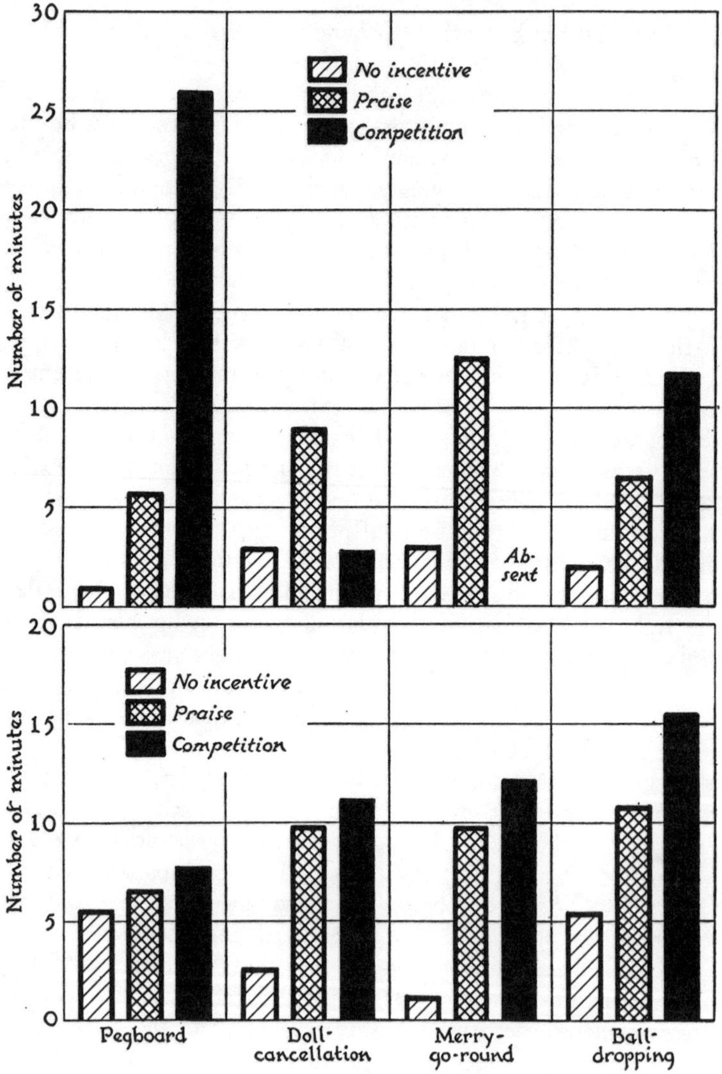

FIGURE 14. — PERFORMANCES OF BD (UPPER) AND GI (LOWER) IN FOUR TEST SITUATIONS

in the no-incentive situation. GI, while persisting only slightly longer than BD, was less easily diverted, talked less, and made no overtures for attention. BD, on the other hand, wanted to enter-

TABLE 39.—RAW SCORES OF SUBJECT BD

TASK	No Incentive		Praise		Competition	
	Persisting Time	Rate	Persisting Time	Rate	Persisting Time	Rate
Pegboard	1.0		5.7		26.0(3)	
Doll-cancellation. .	3.0	1.3	9.0	.8	2.5(1)	1.6
Merry-go-round . .	3.0		12.5		Absent	
Ball-dropping . . .	2.0	9.0	6.6	7.5	11.9(4)	9.3
Total.	9.0		33.8		40.4	

	First Presentation (No Incentive)	Second Presentation (Competition)	Third Presentation (Praise)
Tinker Toy	17.0	22.0(3)	18.5

TABLE 40.—RAW SCORES OF SUBJECT GI

TASK	No Incentive		Praise		Competition	
	Persisting Time	Rate	Persisting Time	Rate	Persisting Time	Rate
Pegboard	5.5		6.25		7.5 (3)*	
Doll-cancellation. .	2.5	1.6	9.8	1.1	11.1 (3)*	1.7
Merry-go-round . .	1.25		9.8		12.25(2)	
Ball-dropping . . .	5.5	23.0	10.75	18.6	15.3 (2.5)	15.0
Total.	14.75		36.6		46.15	

	First Presentation (Competition)	Second Presentation (Praise)	Third Presentation (No Incentive)
Tinker Toy	34.5(3)	16.2	9.0

* Left with two others.

tain his audience. In the kindergarten and also at home he was reported as being more easily diverted than GI and likely to become irritable if he did not receive attention.

As in the case of all the children in this last classification, who showed a high responsiveness to praise and competition, the response of BD and GI to the social stimuli was probably, in part at least, associated with the frequent encouragement and approval they receive for a large number of their activities. All the children in this group are talented in some respect, and undoubtedly their level of self-esteem has been built up by the accumulation of praise received for creditable performances. The raising of this self-esteem undoubtedly stimulates the desire for more praise. The factors associated with the differences between GI and BD may lie partly in the differences in their talents. GI seems to have attained a more mature standing with older people, and she is superior in accom-

TABLE 41.—RAW SCORES OF SUBJECT GB

TASK	NO INCENTIVE		PRAISE		COMPETITION	
	Persisting Time	Rate	Persisting Time	Rate	Persisting Time	Rate
Pegboard	3.5		12.0		20.0(4)	
Doll-cancellation. .	3.0	1.0	3.0	1.3	5.0(4)	1.0
Merry-go-round . .	1.5		8.2		14.0(4)	
Ball-dropping . . .	1.5	20.0	17.2	11.7	4.0(3)	8.0
Total.	9.5		40.4		43.0	

	FIRST PRESENTATION (No Incentive)	SECOND PRESENTATION (Competition)	THIRD PRESENTATION (Praise)
Tinker Toy	15.8	3.0(1.5)	2.7

plishment in many kindergarten tasks. BD is very clever in imaginative and dramatic activities. He may have been so successful in entertaining people with his histrionic talents that he substitutes these activities for the more serious tasks in which GI excels. If this is the case, the more or less irrelevant "entertaining" behavior which BD displayed while carrying on manual activities may have been an attempt to substitute his successful attention-getting talents for activities that did not appeal to him.

BD was more affected by the competitive situation than GI. That this was true not only in the experiment was attested by the kindergarten teachers and the children's mother. It is possible that this condition has grown up because BD has played with his older brothers more frequently and in more kinds of competitive games than his sister has.

Although the raw scores indicate that GB (Table 41) was very uneven in her performances, she is classified in this group because her total praise and competition scores are much higher than her no-incentive scores and because three times she was the last to leave her competitive group. Her performances, however, were more erratic than those of the others in the group. It is interesting that she is the only one in this group whose relations at home are full of conflict. She is one of seven children, and her mother very frankly said that GB annoys her most of the time. Offsetting this conflict, however, is the fact that GB, a talented and appealing child, has won the admiration of her teachers and of an adult neighbor, who "plays with her every day." These satisfying contacts may have compensated to some extent for her home situation, and must have reduced an otherwise high state of unreleased tension that might have led to consistently poor persisting performances.

TABLE 42.—RAW SCORES OF SUBJECT BA

TASK	NO INCENTIVE		PRAISE		COMPETITION	
	Persisting Time	Rate	Persisting Time	Rate	Persisting Time	Rate
Pegboard	1.8		5.8		5.8(3)	
Doll-cancellation. .	4.8	.6	6.3	1.1	37.5(4)	.7
Merry-go-round . .	12.5		12.6		36.0(3)	
Ball-dropping . . .	1.8	15.5	14.5	9.0	11.8(2)	7.6
Total.	20.9		39.2		91.1	

	FIRST PRESENTATION (No Incentive)	SECOND PRESENTATION (Competition)	THIRD PRESENTATION (Praise)
Tinker Toy	32.5	27.8(4)	2.5

The case of subject BA (Table 42) is the example par excellence of the cumulative effect of psychological failure in the Tinker Toy task. This record shows the great drop from his first and second performances with Tinker Toy to his third—from about half an hour to two and a half minutes. Figure 15 gives a graphic picture of his performances in the presentation order. It was evident that BA's level of aspiration for the first two performances was very high. He was "set" to make a complete copy of the model. He handled his work with considerable ability and in the first model, when he was working alone, he completed everything except the proper placing of the pulley belts. Once he called to the experimenter in a high voice, "Miss H, I've got into quite a problem," but he kept at the task assiduously, although the experimenter replied that he must work by himself. Once he almost had the belts in place, but they finally slipped. For eight minutes longer he worked on this part, but again the pulley slipped. This illustrates the extent of his failure.

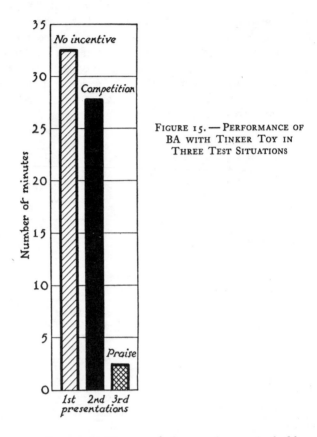

FIGURE 15. — PERFORMANCE OF BA WITH TINKER TOY IN THREE TEST SITUATIONS

In the next, the competitive, performance he worked fifteen minutes longer than his nearest competitor but left the task before he had tried as hard as the time before. In the third performance he stayed just long enough to put together six pieces, although the task was given in the praise situation, which improved his length of activity in the other tasks. He obviously went to the experiment room as a polite concession to the experimenter, and he did this only after considerable urging. Indeed, BA was the exception to the general rule that children were taken to the experiment room only when they were very willing to go. This after-effect of failure apparently did not carry over to any other task. BA's scores on tasks subsequent to the last Tinker Toy performance were as high as fifteen minutes. This experiment was not set up to test this observation properly, but it is an interesting one in the light of Lewin's (28, chapter 2) hypothesis of boundaries between psychological tension systems.

It appears that the motive which gave the strong positive appeal to the Tinker Toy task was the achievement of a goal in a problem-solving task. Although the experimenter suggested to the subject that it would be interesting to try to make a Tinker Toy model like the one before him, there was no compulsion beyond that suggestion. Also, since a number of the children did not attempt to finish a similar model, it seems probable that the goal-setting was determined not by the experimenter but by the child, plus the nature of the task, which was in itself goal-setting. BA's level of aspiration induced a strong need that was not released; twice it was unsatisfied, and we have seen that the psychological failure was profound enough to result in a negative attitude very much stronger than BA's need for social recognition in the praise situation. Perhaps, since the child knew that he was not actually meeting the situation as he saw it, he found the praise irrelevant and misplaced.

It is possible that in addition to BA's high standard for himself with regard to the task his nearness of approach to the goal also heightened his experience of failure. It is reasonable to suppose that proximity to a goal raises the degree of tension, so that its lack of release would bring about a very "annoying" experience. (BA's Tinker Toy performances are schematically represented in Figure 16.)

A clue as to why BA's aspiration was set so high comes from the home questionnaire. He works with tools and constructive materials at home; and at his grandfather's, where he visits often, he has a tool bench of his own. He and his grandfather work together and seriously discuss problems in the *Popular Mechanics* magazine. At both places, his mother reported, BA is always assisted when he is unable to complete anything he has started. In other words, he is finally successful, and has learned to expect to be successful. Indeed, he informed the experimenter that he "got directions for the hard parts" when he made things at home or with his grandfather. In the experiment, of course, he did not. He was told he must work alone, but his previous successes plus his level of ability in problem-solving gave him a reasonable basis for setting the high goal of completion. In BA's case we see the importance of considering factors in the permanent psychobiological field for understanding—or assistance in understanding—behavior in the momentary field.

BA showed the effect of Tinker Toy failure to a greater extent than any of the other children. For those subjects whose third performance was not so early a withdrawal from the field it is probable

FIGURE 16. — DIAGRAM OF CONFLICT
FOR BA IN TEST SITUATION

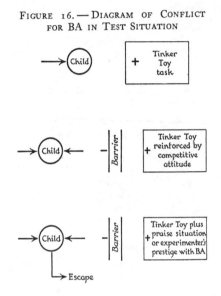

that the first failure had lowered the level of aspiration for the subsequent performances, so that they did not have in the later performances so strong an experience of failure as BA did.

Some explanation of this sort must pertain, for instance, to subject GJ's Tinker Toy performance. Her raw scores for the Tinker Toy, shown in Table 43 and Figure 17, indicate, to be sure, a very great drop from the first to the second and third performances, but neither of these last two is nearly so brief as BA's third. The report on GJ given just below shows that her first performance was very strongly motivated by the goal of completing the model. Perhaps then, it is surprising that she stayed as long as she did for the second and third trials. But possibly the accompaniment of praise reduced the effect of the first failure; or GJ may have recognized the limitations of her ability, since she was very unsuccessful even after trying for sixty-five minutes, and frequently reiterated, "Well, I don't know how I am going to get this done!" Such a recognition would tend to reduce her level of aspiration. It is again obvious that only systematic variation of the several conditions indicated can determine how this aspiration level is related to successive performances.

TABLE 43.—RAW SCORES OF SUBJECT GJ*

TASK	No Incentive		Praise		Competition	
	Persisting Time	Rate	Persisting Time	Rate	Persisting Time	Rate
Pegboard	5.25		22.5		12.0(4)	
Doll-cancellation	8.25	.9	6.0	.7	18.0(1)	.6
Merry-go-round	6.6		45.0		58.0(3)	
Total	20.0		73.5		88.0	

	First Presentation (Praise)	Second Presentation (No Incentive)	Third Presentation (Competition)
Tinker Toy	65.0	11.5	14.6(1)

* GJ left school before the ball-dropping task.

Subject GJ is an interesting case, not particularly for her responses to the incentives, but as a striking instance of a child with a tremendous drive for setting and achieving a goal. Her need for this is indicated primarily by her Tinker Toy and pegboard performances. Her merry-go-round performance was also outstanding for its duration. The nature of this task makes it impossible to relate this duration to any particular goal-setting with respect to the task itself, but there is evidence that with this task GJ set out to win in the competitive situation.

GJ's first Tinker Toy performance, with praise, earned for her the highest score in the entire experiment, regardless of the task or incentive situation. Her resolute intention to finish the task is evident from a sample of her conversation. She was making very poor headway, and was constantly baffled as to what to do next. Once, after she had sat still merely looking at the model for more than sixty seconds, so that the experimenter reminded her that she could leave if she wished, she replied in a determined tone, "Don't keep telling me I can stop. I know it. . . . I am not going

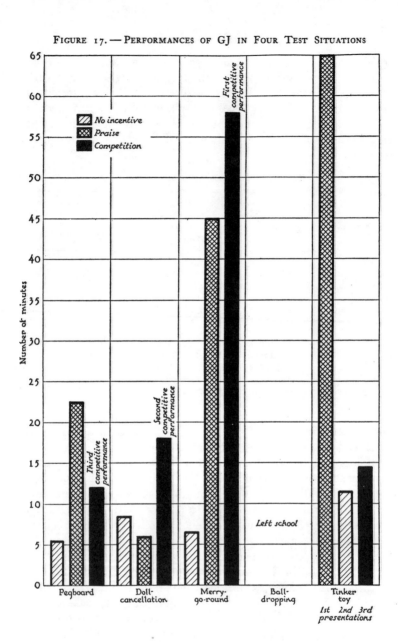

FIGURE 17. — PERFORMANCES OF GJ IN FOUR TEST SITUATIONS

to stop until I get this all done, if I can't come back to finish it tomorrow. I don't want something that's not finished!" Her merry-go-round performances were very long, in spite of noticeable weariness. In the competitive group she stayed for fifty-eight minutes, although after thirty-nine minutes she seemed weary and bored. She kept on "because it's fun," in her words, but one factor was clearly her desire to win.

In supplement to the Tinker Toy illustrations, an analysis of her total merry-go-round performance suggests the relation of failure to the effectiveness of incentives for persisting behavior, as well as adding evidence to the picture of GJ as a mighty "goal-driver." In spite of her very long and tiring effort to win at the merry-go-round, she did *not* win, and in her subsequent competitive performances we see evidence of the extent of the psychological effect of this failure. It appears possible that failure produced a strong enough negative response to the competitive situation to counterbalance the positive desire for recognition aroused by that situation. In the competitive situation following that with the merry-go-round (the doll-cancellation task) she was first to leave; in the next (pegboard) she was fourth, but had to remain only twelve minutes to achieve that place; and in the Tinker Toy she was again first to leave. But what of the subsequent merry-go-round performances? We should expect to see their duration fall off immediately too, since she failed to win, but her second performance (with praise) was forty-five minutes long. The third, carried on alone, was only 6.5 minutes, but this was 4.5 minutes above the median for this situation.

For GJ, then, it seems possible that the goal object is not "dynamically" related to the total situation but is rather quite specific. We may guess that her goal was not essentially to win at the merry-go-round, but to win. The failure, therefore, was apparently attached to the not-winning rather than to the task. This nonintegration is not so apparent with regard to BE and BG, the other long performers in GJ's competitive group. We have seen that BE won, with a sixty-minute performance, and that BG, although leaving second, stayed fifty-two minutes. Their second performances with this same task dropped to 12.5 and 9.0 minutes respectively, but their subsequent *competitive* performances were higher than GJ's. It is possible, though certainly not self-evident—because praise was not consistently effective for BG and BE—that the whole performance was more integrated for them (Lewin would say that the dynamic wall between the two parts of the situation was thinner for them) than for GJ, so that the merry-go-round performance took on some of the negative effect of the total wearisome situation, thus affecting their later performances in this specific task.

It would appear, further, that GJ's tension toward a goal was so potent as to be capable, perhaps of isolating itself from, certainly of dominating, other simultaneous tension systems. Although she did not make outstanding records with the doll-cancellation, yet her performance indicates that she was determined to carry on beyond the stage of pleasure in the task, or, we may say, beyond her satiation point. For instance, the following are some of the records taken by the experimenter: "Works at coloring special parts of the dolls, then finishes page with single cancellation lines.—Sighs and fingers over sheets not done, turns pages over slowly, examines them, and colors figures on back of page.—Takes a long time looking over completed sheet. Fingers sheets she has finished. Is there a self-set goal? [E set this question when GJ was not familiar to her.]—Colored five kites and leaves in solid color."

Because of this extraneous behavior the experimenter suggested more than once that GJ could go; but this only gave her new impetus. Her various methods of working with the material enabled her to keep at the task, which she was determined to do. Something was furnishing a drive for her to continue; there was some sort of self-imposed goal.

The evidence for her goal-driving motivation is most strikingly illustrated by her pegboard performances. The pegboard, as already stated, had thirty-seven holes in each row. Many of the children indicated that they had a loosely defined goal by saying, "I am going to do two more," or even, "I am going to do twenty-five." This goal was often very fluid, however, since they would not stop at the "two more," but would often go on, with or without another verbally expressed goal. In only eighteen of the sixty-eight pegboard performances (eight represent repetitions of the initial performances made to test reliability) was a whole row or some multiple of a row completed. Of these eighteen performances, GJ made four. Every time she came to the pegboard she finished either one or two complete rows. No other child did this more than twice, and most of those who finished a row at all did so only once. GJ's pegboard performance was as follows: first presentation (praise), 74 pegs (two rows) put in; second presentation (repetition of first—praise), 37 pegs (one row) put in; third presentation (no incentive), 37 pegs (one row) put in; fourth presentation (competition), 74 pegs (two rows) put in.

GJ's conversation is very important in illustrating how strong this goal-setting and striving was. The first time she showed considerable interest in where the experimenter had obtained the board, why there were yellow-headed pegs, how many holes there were in the board, and especially how many pegs she had put in. "What if I do the whole thing?" she queried. When the experimenter replied that it would take a long time, she said, "I don't care. Maybe I will do just two rows," which she did.

The following day she was brought in to repeat the task. She greeted it with this remark, spoken with determination, "I am only going to do one row this time. . . . It's no fun to do the same thing. I want to do some on my rocking chair. If I don't get back [to the kindergarten] in time, I will only do part of a row next time." Absolutely nothing had been said about finishing a row; these were GJ's own reactions to the materials. And in spite of the remark indicating that she had had enough of that task the first day, she immediately stated her intention of finishing a row. She seemed obviously annoyed, moreover, because there were so many holes. She had asked who made the holes. "Why did he [the technician] make so many holes? The children don't do so many holes. Why *did* he? If they [the children] did, they would have to begin early, as soon as they get their wraps off." Later she said, "I am only going to do one row. How many will I have done when I get the whole row done? How many if I did all these holes?" Then again a little later. "He didn't need to make so many [holes]. He could have made this many" (indicating a distance on the board). Before she stopped she once more said with feeling, "He didn't need to make so many!"

A strong conflict was apparent between GJ's desire to finish this thing and the practical impossibility of doing it. If "he" hadn't made so many holes she could have had some hope of finishing. About five weeks passed before she came to the pegboard again. This time she was working alone; she made no remarks, merely hummed to herself while she completed one row. About a month later still, when the task was reinforced with the competitive situation, she finished two rows. GJ left school and did not do the ball-dropping series. In all the others, however, she gave indications of a drive which seems to pervade a very large area of her activities.

GJ's record in the experiment is bulwarked by what the kindergarten teachers tell us. They rate her very high in persisting behavior, that is, in being seldom diverted by other occurrences and "carrying on" until an activity is completed. Her rate of accomplishment, however, both in the experiment and in the kindergarten, is average or below. She is the determined plodder. Her mother reports that at home GJ keeps hard at work at difficult tasks in spite of baffling situations, murmuring to herself, "If a task is once begun, never leave it till it's done." One wonders just how much of a behavior-determinant this slogan may be in her general activities.

GJ is an extreme case, at least within the bounds of this study, exhibiting a drive to complete what she starts and to make a goal where none has been set by the nature of the situation. This drive in her case is a fundamental motivation for her persisting behavior. We are unable for the most part to determine the degree—or even sometimes the presence—of goal-setting among most of the subjects in the present study. As we have said, however, their conversations reveal various evidences of it. It may be that there are different degrees of goal-setting among individuals, and it also seems highly probable that this drive is a fundamental motive for persisting behavior in various situations. Its strength could be tested only in a series of activities encompassing different kinds of tasks and different degrees of difficulty and completeness.

SUMMARY OF FINDINGS

In this analysis of individual cases, we find indications that the effect of incentives upon persisting behavior is dependent upon such factors as the level of aspiration to reach a goal, success and failure, the specific nature of the incentives imposed and the activities performed, social relations, the psychological processes of substitution or rationalization, and the conflict of tension systems.

We have seen the varying degrees of psychological effect produced both in the Tinker Toy task and in the competitive situation regardless of the task. For some subjects, their brief performances with the Tinker Toy suggest that they did not determine to reach the goal of completing the model. For others, the idea of finishing was either immediate or grew with their progress in the construction. (Subjects BA and GJ illustrate the former; BB and GA the latter.)

The degree of psychological failure appears to be dependent upon the definiteness of the goal-setting and the subsequent failure to reach the goal. In the cases in which the effect of failure seemed profound, it appears that in the conflict between the negative effect of the failure and the positive effect of the accompanying incentive the failure was the stronger. That a generally high level of self-confidence toward probem-solving ability might weaken the effect of a single or even a repeated failure—as a substitute satisfaction for the momentary failure—is suggested by the fact that BB and GA, who showed goal-setting attitudes but only a moderate effect of failure, are rated as superior in problem-solving. It is possible, then, that the teachers who so rated them, as well as other adults, provide them with a secure and stable reputation for high accomplishment that is not easily disrupted by incidental failures. The degree of psychological failure appears to be related to very broad aspects of personality.

The experience of failure or success in competing with a group has been indicated in several instances. It is illustrated most strikingly by the performances of BE and GJ. For BE the situation was regarded as representing both the positive element of winning at the merry-go-round and the negative one of fatigue and satiation. For GJ it appeared to represent only the strong negative effect of failure to attain her goal, plus fatigue and satiation combined. The effect upon both these subjects was that they never again stayed so long in a competitive situation. On the basis of merely observing the factors in the situation the writer hazards the suggestion that for BE the first experience sufficed as a substitute for the effort necessary to win in other competitive situations. For GJ, however, she suggests that a quite different process occurred, because the effect was entirely one of failure.

The case of subject BE, as well as those cases illustrating progressive changes after previous failure in the Tinker Toy task, is good evidence for the view that the law of effect as usually stated is too simple. The implication of the law stated in terms of positive and negative behavior (it is not necessary to consider the controversy concerning the use of the experiential terms of satisfaction and annoyance, etc.) would seem to be that any activity being carried on is motivated by a single need; that when the organism is "approaching the situation" it is because the effect is positive, and when "retreating" it is because the effect is negative. But when the individual organism is observed in a field-force area there is evidence that the needs are multiple; that the tension systems, by which we have chosen to represent the needs, are acting in different degrees of strength and perhaps in quite different directions at the same time.

Let us look at the example of the child striving for a piece of candy, but for whom a barrier has been raised against his obtaining it (28, chapter 3). We find that it is not until this child has failed several times that he leaves the field (provided he does not find the way around the barrier). After the first failure, perhaps the second or third, his behavior is still positive, although modified. That is, if the goal object is not changed in position or demand value—by the addition of more candy, let us say—the child's behavior in its direction will be of shorter duration and of a less energetic quality. Presumably the behavior has been changed by the effects of failure, although it is still positive with respect to the goal object. The point is that both the positive and the negative elements are represented in the single response. Lewin's concept of tension systems, with some tensions positive and some negative in respect to the goal activity, indicates the necessity for positing behavior as the result of various tensions.

It seems evident that a series of comparatively similar incentive situations are functionally related to one another, and the closeness and nature of the relationship depends, among other things, on the degree of psychological failure or success experienced in them.

Among some of the subjects we found that specificity in the incentive situations was a factor in the effectiveness of the incentive. GC and BE, for example, both showed a minimal or ambiguous responsiveness to praise, and it appeared that their attitudes toward the experimenter accounted in part for this condition. For at least four subjects, also, the teacher reported that moderate rather than enthusiastic praise was the most effective. It has been pointed out that social experiences may have determined these attitudes. The kindergarten teacher reported that a competitive situation set up by the children was sometimes effective, whereas one set up by the teacher was not. Undoubtedly the psychological relation of the individual to the various members of the competitive group would also be found to be a significant variable, but this factor was not evident in the present study.

A major factor affecting generally high or low persisters, as they were classified roughly in disregard of many limiting factors in any such classification, seems to lie in social relations. The high persisters seem to have adequate opportunities for satisfying the need for free manipulative activity, while some of the low performers are restricted in such activity by social conflict in their homes, or on the other hand are too much praised for nonproductive activities. The subjects in the classification showing high response to praise and competition have been cited as examples of those who work and play at home in a social atmosphere of some understanding and encouragement. But in the homes of BI and BH, the former a consistently low performer in duration of activity, the latter a consistently restless and easily diverted one, the experimenter found rather striking examples of social conflict. GB also indicated fundamental conflict at home, and her behavior was erratic and inconsistent in spite of the fact that she was among those highly affected by praise and competition. (We have no data that give us an opportunity to point out negative cases or exceptions to this observation of the relation of conflict to persisting behavior.)

Among subjects GG, GD, GF, and GH, who also belong in the "low" classification, we do not find evidences of fundamental conflict (although we do not deny that it may exist) but rather of "babying" and overindulgence by adults. The home reports on these four children indicate that each of them is petted, spoiled, and otherwise coddled, so that it seems reasonable to suppose that the demands made upon them are below the level of their abilities. This would mean that poor or inadequate performances are accompanied by a degree of satisfaction great enough to substitute for lack of accomplishment in more effortful activities. It is interesting, also, that for none of these four children did the mothers report any interest in difficult tasks. The children were primarily interested in dramatic or motor plays, and "made only simple things." The kindergarten teachers concurred in this report. A comparison between the highs and the lows in our group, then, suggests that there is some relationship between performance in manipulatory activities and the level of the demands of adults in the home situation. It appears that a more or less generally high level of persisting behavior is dependent among other things upon an adequate balance between the child's ability and the level of performance that brings him approval and praise; and that a low level, as shown by a short activity span or by erratic behavior, depends upon a performance demand that deviates too far from his ability in either direction.

THE APPARENT BASIS OF MOTIVATED BEHAVIOR

Very little light has been cast on the nature of the motives for such behavior as we have described. Yet it should again be pointed out in regard to the effectiveness of incentives upon persisting behavior that—as Lewin has shown for other behavior processes—the behavior is the result not of any single motive or need, but rather of a number of such needs, which may act to reinforce or to oppose the primary goal-directed activity of the organism. In this matter, the psychological hypotheses of tension systems, resultant of tension systems, conflict and substitution, and experience have been very useful.

To say, as the literature commonly does, that praise and competition "satisfy an urge to excel, a need for recognition," is merely using the layman's unanalytical terms to express what we observe, but as yet our ignorance of the processes involved makes no better terms available. Leuba (27), in discussing the effectiveness of incentives, has suggested that, given the fundamental urge that is satisfied by a praise incentive, the number of situations that can arouse the incentive attitude is increased by conditioning. "At first the child may exert himself only for praise, toys, and delicacies," he states, "but if he gets these when he outdoes others in competitive performances, the presence of others performing the same task, or the sight of their scores, may become eventually effective stimuli for the incentive attitude; or the mere sight of his own scores, irrespective of those of others, may come to stimulate that attitude, and finally perhaps the work alone will suffice to do so." The developmental process of the incentive attitudes, however, is at the present time entirely hypothetical.

In regard to the motives for behavior that persist in the absence of any external incentive other than the task to which orientation is maintained, we may posit several hypotheses. It is reasonable to consider conditioning, as Leuba has described it, as the "motive" in the case of the use of some materials. Undoubtedly proprioceptive inertia, the psychological "line of least resistance," sometimes operates, although with manipulative materials requiring some adaptation to the special characteristics of their structure this operation would probably be minimal. It appears from evidence of various kinds and most notably from the work of Zeigarnik and Ovsiankina (28, pages 242–44), that a need for completing a task or achieving a goal may be considered a fundamental motive. Closely related to this—perhaps only another aspect of the same motive—is the need for *setting* a goal to achieve, whether or not one exists in the nature of the task. The present study suggests that this goal-setting need may exist among individuals in various degrees of strength.

Still another aspect of what is probably this same motive toward goal-setting and goal-achieving is the tendency that Heidbreder (18) observed among children—that of seeing a new situation as a problem and attempting to solve it. In her experiment she presented the subject with three boxes in one of which a doll was concealed. The problem consisted of the subject's discovering the principle of relationship among the boxes that would always give him the clue to finding the doll. School-age children and adults reacted to her experimental situation as a definite problem, even when there were no specific instructions from the experimenter. Heidbreder concludes: "Certain situations can be counted on to produce the thought response in human beings . . . just as there are others which in most cases elicit the responses commonly classified as reflex, emotional, instinctive, and habitual behavior." For her older subjects the material was understandable in terms of achieving a goal. It is possible that this was as fundamental to their reaction as their seeing in the situation an intellectual problem.

Social factors also may have been associated with the no-incentive persisting behavior. The habit of working alone, although it did not appear in the home records of the longer persisters, may have influenced the performance. Docility, too, may have played a small part; in spite of the freedom to leave when they wanted to, some of these children might already have become conditioned to adult suggestion so that they would continue their performances for a short time under its influence. Finally, some children may have voluntarily added factors of imaginative play which would lend the material alone an added attractiveness.

Investigations such as that of Cushing (9), which concludes, primarily on the basis of tetrad differences, that "occupations . . . which involve manipulative materials of a simple repetitive sort" are reducible to a common factor plus small group factors, suggest that "persistence" or "perseveration" is basically a *constant* (compare Carr, 6), native to or physiologically inherent in the specific organism and presumably constituting the "motive" for persisting behavior. We have not tested this possibility in the present study except as our inter-rho's, particularly in the no-incentive situation, are positive, although moderate or low. However this may be, our material, while not determining irrevocably any particular relationship, has pointed conclusively to the fact that any fundamental or inherent basis for a constant or universal factor of persisting behavior (by whatever name) is very definitely limited by variable conditions both in the momentary and more permanent areas of the psychological environment. And these variable conditions are co-existent with the problems of the changing needs and the experience of the individual.

VI. SUMMARY AND CONCLUSIONS

Within the limits of the present study, the effectiveness of incentive situations increased for the group in the following order: first, task carried on without further incentive; second, with the praise of the experimenter; and third, with a group of four children among whom a competitive attitude was promoted by the experimenter. This order held in four of the five tasks presented, as well as for the total scores of all the tasks. In these four tasks no end or goal was set by the type of task, and they all offered either visual or kinesthetic evidence of the progress attained.

Not only the order but also the relative degree to which each incentive was effective varied with the nature of the task. In the no-incentive situation the subjects quickly had enough of the merry-go-round, while, except for the special case of the Tinker Toy, the fine motor skill required by the pegboard attracted them the longest. With praise and competition there was a change in this order. Praise was considerably more effective with the merry-go-round—requiring large-muscle motor skill—than with the other three tasks, which were but slightly differentiated in median activity spans under praise. Competition, as compared with praise and with no incentive, showed a greater influence upon the merry-go-round than upon the other tasks. Competition also affected the two simple, repetitive tasks of doll-cancellation and ball-dropping more than it did the precise, finely coordinated, and therefore more fatiguing task of the pegboard. We conclude that the effectiveness of incentives is limited by the nature of the task performed.

This conclusion is further corroborated by the fact that the foregoing incentive order did not hold for the Tinker Toy, a difficult construction problem presenting in its own structure a definite goal. For this task the case studies indicate that certain conditions were functionally more closely related to duration of activity than were the incentives; these conditions existed in individual attitudes, indicating that each performance did not function separately, but rather in a close psychological unity with the subject's previous experiences with the materials. These attitudes, in turn, are to be understood not only from factors in the experimental stimulus field, but also from those in the more permanent social environment. The attitude that seems primarily related to the scores in the three Tinker Toy trials is the degree of psychological failure experienced in not achieving the goal that was voluntarily set. From the individual cases it appears that the strength of the failure experience is related, among other things, to the individual's level of aspiration toward achieving the goal, to his general level of self-confidence with regard to problem-solving activities, possibly to the degree of amelioration of the failure experience when the activity was accompanied by praise or competition, and to certain other social experiences.

In the cases where there was some consistency in the responses to the incentives, these responses appeared to be related to habitual attitudes probably determined by social experiences of long standing. The case studies show that the effectiveness of competition is related to the level of aspiration for winning, to accomplishment in comparison with that of the competitors, and, in a series of competitive situations, in some cases to the substitution of one successful competitive experience for later ones. There is evidence that rationalization may complicate an individual's responses to a given incentive situation.

The factors of sex, socio-economic status, age, and intelligence quotient were examined, but they gave a very unsatisfactory basis for understanding the individual differences in persisting-time scores. An examination of the psychological field of each subject presented more significant relationships.

It is concluded that a generally high level of persisting behavior is dependent, among other things, upon a level of performance demand from adults that is properly adjusted to the child's ability. The factors associated with more or less consistently short performances appear to be two opposite conditions in the permanent social environments of the children. There seem to be on the one hand unreasonable demands by adults and on the other insufficient demands. In the first case the unwarranted expectations and irritable demands seem to bring about a lack of confidence or at least to interfere with free-play expression. It is posited that this condition sets up a general state of tension from which the child tries to escape and of which his restless behavior is a symptom. In the second case approval is lavishly bestowed upon effortless activity, personal attractiveness, or some specialized talent, so that this approval seems to function as a substitute for any need of recognition for effortful manual activities.

The results of this study suggest that persisting behavior is both general and specific. There is a low but positive relationship between persisting performances in different tasks and different incentive situations. Analysis shows that consistency of performance between the tasks and the situations is more typical of some individuals than of others. What one investigator might see as evidence for a common factor plus small group factors, however, may be expressed otherwise by saying that, while persisting behavior may be somewhat consistent from one situation to another, it is nevertheless highly dependent upon several variables. Significant among these are the kind of task, the specific conditions of the incentive situations, and broad personality characteristics that affect the subjects' attitudes toward the various situations.

The present study has obviously been an exploratory one. It has indicated, however, that persisting behavior and the effect of incentives upon it are related to very pervasive aspects of personality. These aspects are the effects of demonstrable conditions in both the immediate and the permanent psychological environments of the children. In other words, it appears that persisting behavior and motivation (in the form of incentives) are, in part at least, *learning* problems. Therefore, longitudinal or long-sectional studies and studies of the cumulative effects of performance are essential to an understanding of these behavior patterns.

APPENDIX I
DRAMATIS PERSONAE

SUBJECT	SEX	AGE Years	AGE Months	INTELLIGENCE QUOTIENT	NUMBER, SEX, AGE OF SIBLINGS	APPROXIMATE NUMBER MONTHS IN NURSERY SCHOOL	APPROXIMATE NUMBER MONTHS IN KINDERGARTEN	SOCIO-ECONOMIC STATUS	FATHER'S EDUCATION	FATHER'S OCCUPATION	MOTHER'S EDUCATION
GI*	f	5	3	139	1f, 13 years; 2m, 11 years; 1m, 5 years	1	1	I	Ph. D.	University professor	High school
BD*	m	5	3	121	1f, 13 years; 2m, 11 years; 1f, 5 years	1	1	I	Ph. D.	University professor	High school
BA	m	6	0	116	1f, 3½ years	None	7	I	Ph. D.	University professor	3 years college
BI	m	5	11	100	1f, 25 years; 1f, 16 years; 1m, 14 years	None	12	III	4 years high school and business college	Salesman (unemployed)	4 years high school
GD	f	4	10	100	2m, 15 years; 1f, 13 years; 1m, 3 years	12	1	III	No information	Salesman	No information
BB	m	5	1	130	1m, 11 years; 1m, 8 years	None	1	I	M. D.	Director of hospital	4 years college
GE	f	4	11	108	1m, 3½ years; 1f, 17 months	12	1	IV	8th grade	Bundle checker	1 year high school
GJ	f	5	11	106	1m, 4 years	None	4	IV	4 years college	In hospital for illness	4 years college

* GI and BD are twins.

DRAMATIS PERSONAE—Continued

		5	7			25 (?)	1	IV	6th grade	Motorman	8th grade
GK. . .	f	5	7	108	1m, 9½ years; 1f, 7½ years; 1m, 6½ years; 1m, 4 years	None	2	I	M. Sc.	University professor	4 years music after high school
BH. . .	m	5	2	125	1m, 2 years	21	4	III	8th grade (technical school)	Bank clerk	2 years high school
GG. . .	f	5	5	119	1m, 8½ years	21	1	II	3 years high school	Bank auditor	8th grade
BC. . .	m	5	2	117	1f, 7 years; 1f, 3 years	21	9	V	8th grade	Truck driver	8th grade
BG. . .	m	5	8	100	1m, 4½ years	None	8	I	Ph. D.	University professor	4 years college
GA. . .	f	5	4	117	1f, 11 years; 1f, 7½ years	9	5	II	4 years high school	Owner tire shop	3 years high school
GH. . .	f	5	8	100	1f, 11 years; 1f, 9 years	21	5	II	2 years college	Assistant credit manager	1 year graduate work
GC. . .	f	5	5	115	1m, 4 years	None	5	III	High school	Manager gas station	3 years college
GF. . .	f	5	11	110	None	None	6	III	No information†	No information†	8th grade and business college
BF. . .	m	5	11	117	1f, 8½ years	21	9	V	3 years high school	Sewer at milling company	4 years normal
BE. . .	m	5	10	117	None	None	1	II	2 years high school	Accountant	4 years high school
GB. . .	f	4	9	130	1m, 17½ years; 1m, 13 years; 1f, 12 years; 1f, 10 years; 1m, 9 years; 1m, baby						

† Parents separated.

APPENDIX II

HOME QUESTIONNAIRE
(Filled out with mother of child)
I. GENERAL INFORMATION

Child's name_____ Date_____
Mother's education_____Mother's birthplace_____ Age____
Father's education_____Father's birthplace_____ Age____
Are parents separated?_____ Divorced?_____ Father's occupation_____
Child's attendance at nursery school_____ Kindergarten_____
Age and sex of siblings_____

II. COMPANIONS

1. How many children are there in the neighborhood with whom child plays three or four times a week?_____ Ages and sex_____
2. Does child play alone O__ Occ__ S__ N__ DK__?*
3. Does he lead other children O__ Occ__ S__ N__ DK__?
4. Has mother played with child since last (a week ago)?_____
If so, about how many times? _____ Nature of play:_____
5. Has father played with child since last (a week ago)?_____
If so, about how many times?_____ Nature of play:_____
6. Have other adults played with child since last (a week ago)?_____
If so, about how many times?_____ Nature of play:_____
Relation of these adults to child?_____
7. Do playmates come into the home O__ Occ__ S__ N__? Does child play in other homes O__ Occ__ S__ N__?

III. MATERIALS AND BEHAVIOR

8. What toys are in the home? (List read to parent to aid recall.)
9. What does child play with at least twice a week? (Check with cross.)
10. What does child play with four or five times a week? (Underline.)
11. Does he think of ways to occupy himself O__ Occ__ S__ N__ DK__? Rely on adult O__ Occ__ S__ N__? Rely on other children O__ Occ__ S__ N__?
12. When a task in construction or handwork is difficult for the child, does he leave it after a short trial O__ Occ__ S__ N__ DK__? Does he stick to it until he has tried many times to solve it O__ Occ__ S__ N__ DK__?
13. What activities are there for which he carries over an eager interest from season to season?
14. Does he carry on the same kind of activity for three or more days in succession? Describe:
15. Does he ask adult for help O__ Occ__ S__ N__? Describe:
16. If he starts to make something which can be finished in one day, does he complete it O__ Occ__ S__ N__ DK__?
17. Does he stop his work to attend to other things O__ Occ__ S__ N__ DK__? Note any outstanding exceptions:

* These letters stand for the following words: Often, Occasionally, Seldom, Never, Does Not Know.

18. Does child show evidence of a competitive spirit, that is, an effort to "beat" someone else O__ Occ__ S__ N__ DK__? Describe instances:
19. During the last six months what has the child attended to for a particularly long period of time (three or four hours)?
20. Does child ask for praise for his performance O__ Occ__ S__ N__? Does he show other methods of trying to get attention? Describe:
21. When playing with other children does child make suggestions concerning the play O__ Occ__ S__ N__ DK__?

IV. SUPERVISION

22. Does mother have to restrict child's play O__ Occ__ S__ N__? For what reasons?
23. Does child's play irritate mother O__ Occ__ S__ N__? Under what circumstances?
24. Which of the following methods does the mother use in handling the child with respect to his play activities? Designate with O, Occ, S, N.
Praise and encouragement____ Scolding____ Bribing (giving reward for certain behavior)____ Comparison with another child (favorable or unfavorable)____ Corporal punishment____ Making child finish one thing before undertaking another____ Constructive criticism____ Parallel activity with child____ Showing indications of interest voluntarily____ Correction in humorous vein____ Negative criticism____ Indirect suggestion by adult's own performance____. Other methods:
25. Do older children or adults let the child win when they play with him? O__ Occ__ S__ N__? Describe instances of play:
26. For what tasks about the house does the child have responsibility?

Directions Accompanying Teacher's Rating Scale

This rating scale is intended to analyze factors included in and influencing five-year-old children's persisting behavior. It was made particularly for the purpose of obtaining the appraisals of kindergarten teachers. I shall appreciate as careful a rating as you can give.

There are three kinds of activity to be rated—problem-solving, automatic activities, motor skills—in each of several aspects of the child's performance of them. (These activities are defined on the sheets.) The complete rating scale includes three sheets for each child, one for each activity mentioned above, but only one at a time will be given to you.

DIRECTIONS

You will find the names of the children to be rated at the top of the sheets. Read a whole sheet before making your first rating on any kind of activity. This will make your ratings more accurate, and will facilitate other ratings on the same activity.

Consider each roman numeral item separately, trying not to let your judgment on one determine that on another.

It may be of assistance to the rater to know that the middle term under each roman numeral (number 3 where there are five; number 2 where there are three) is assumed to be the *average* performance for the children in the university kindergarten.

In rating a child on a given type of activity, consider the number of activities of that type in which he participates. For example, rate the child's behavior as it occurs in the greatest number of problem-solving activities in which he participates. Do not rate him on one in which his performance is very widely divergent from that in other problem-solving activities.

Please do not consult anyone else on the factors to be rated.

SAMPLE OF TEACHER'S RATING SHEET

Child's Name_____ Rated by_____ Date_____

MOTOR SKILLS*

(Activities in which the child is learning a new motor skill, such as skipping rope, shooting at a target, working on the jungle gym, etc.)

Number that
best describes
child's
behavior

I. Attention: (The word *diverted* implies either stopping work or looking around.) 1. Almost never diverted by other occurrences; 2. Diverted only by very unusual occurrences; 3. Diverted by normally interesting occurrences; 4. Easily diverted by many occurrences; 5. Shifts attention from task continually.   _____

II. Staying qualities (permanence of interest over several weeks): 1. Tries activity every day until skilled; 2. Ceases to try only when difficulty appears great; 3. Ceases to try after several attempts; 4. Ceases to try after a few trials; 5. Does not try more than once or twice.   _____

III. Ability in motor skills: 1. Superior performance; 2. Good performance; 3. Average performance; 4. Poor performance; 5. Very poor performance.   _____

IV. Originality: 1. Almost always attacks activity with individual ideas; 2. Very often presents individual ideas; 3. Shows average originality; 4. Usually relies upon suggestions of others; 5. Relies upon suggestions for every step.   _____

V. Necessity for adult supervision: Child works at his usual performance in this activity 1. With little or no supervision; 2. With occasional supervision; 3. With constant supervision.   _____

VI. Consistency of performance in motor skills: Behavior in activities rated above 1. Is very generally as rated; 2. Varies greatly for different kinds of motor skills.   _____

VII. Kinds of supervision or motivation which most influence the child's performance. Please list the kinds of incentives which affect this child *most* and *least* with regard to his persistence at the task and the quality of his performance. A list of fifteen possible incentive situations is enclosed for your convenience. [This list is given below.]

SUPPLEMENTARY SHEET FOR TEACHER'S RATING SCHEDULE
IN PERSISTING BEHAVIOR

To facilitate your ratings on the item concerning supervision or motivation on the rating schedule, the following suggestions may be of assistance to you. You may use these numbers in making out item VII, if the descriptions adequately express your own meanings.

1. Parallel work—adult working at same table with children and carrying on an activity similar to that of the children.

2. Parallel work—children in group working on similar activities.

3. Individual praise and approval from teacher—either initiated by teacher or definitely sought by child.

4. Reproof from teacher—definite negative disapproval, or scolding.

* A very similar rating sheet was used for the problem-solving and automatic activities.

5. Individual definite suggestions and help in making a better product.
6. Individual positive urging, e.g. "You'd better hurry. It's getting near the end of the work period."
7. Individual correction or suggestion in humorous vein.
8. Teacher's comparison with child's own previous performances.
9. Teacher's comparison of performance of one child with that of another.
10. Competitive situation set up by teacher or children.
11. Insistence upon child's finishing one task before beginning another.
12. Helping child make decisions about work.
13. Group approval initiated in group meeting.
14. Group disapproval or criticism.
15. Teacher's setting goal for product.

Please feel free to add any other types of incentive which you consider important. These are only suggestions.

BIBLIOGRAPHY

1. ANDERSON, H. H., and R. S. SMITH. Motivation of young children: the constancy of certain behavior patterns. Journal of Experimental Education, 2:138–59 (1933).
2. BERTRAND, F.-L. Contribution à l'étude psycho-génétique de l'attention. L'année psychologique, 26:155–58 (1925).
3. BESTOR, M. F. A study of attention in young children. Child Development, 5:368–80 (1934).
4. BILLS, A. G. General experimental psychology. Longmans, Green, and Co., New York, 1934. x + 620 pp.
5. BROWN, M. Continuous reaction as a measure of attention. Child Development, 1:255–91 (1930).
6. CARR, H. The quest for constants. Psychological Review, 40:514–32 (1933).
7. CHASE, L. Motivation of young children, an experimental study of the influence of certain types of external incentives upon the performance of a task (University of Iowa Studies in Child Welfare, Vol. V, No. 3). University of Iowa, 1932.
8. CRUTCHER, R. An experimental study of persistence. Journal of Applied Psychology, 18:409–17 (1934).
9. CUSHING, H. M. A perseverative tendency in preschool children. (Archives of Psychology, Vol. XVII, No. 108). 1929.
10. DALLENBACH, K. M. Attention. Psychological Bulletin, 25:493–512 (1928).
11. DISERENS, C. M., and J. VAUGHN. The experimental psychology of motivation. Psychological Bulletin, 28:15–65 (1931).
12. FAJANS, S. Erfolg, Ausdauer, und Aktivität beim Säugling und Kleinkind. Psychologische Forschungen, 17:268–305 (1933).
13. GEISSLER, L. R. The measurement of attention. American Journal of Psychology, 20:473–529 (1909).
14. GOODENOUGH, F. L., and J. E. ANDERSON. Experimental child study. Century Co., New York, 1931. xii + 546 pp.
15. GOODENOUGH, F. L., and C. R. BRIAN. Certain factors underlying the acquisition of motor skill by preschool children. Journal of Experimental Psychology, 12:127–55 (1929).
16. GREENBERG, P. J. Competition in children. American Journal of Psychology, 44:221–48 (1932).
17. HARTSHORNE, H., M. A. MAY, and J. B. MALLER. Studies in the nature of character: II. Studies in service and self-control. Macmillan Co., New York, 1929.
18. HEIDBREDER, E. F. Problem solving in children and adults. Journal of Genetic Psychology, 35:522–45 (1928).
19. HERRING, A., and H. L. KOCH. A study of some factors influencing the interest span of preschool children. Journal of Genetic Psychology, 38:249–79 (1930).
20. HICKS, J. A. The acquisition of motor skill in young children (University of Iowa Studies in Child Welfare, Vol. IV, No. 5). University of Iowa, 1931.
21. HOPPE, F. Erfolg und Misserfolg. Psychologische Forschungen, 14:1–62 (1930).
22. HURLOCK, E. B. The value of praise and reproof as incentives for children (Archives of Psychology, Vol. XI, No. 71). 1924.

23. JACK, L. M. Behavior of the preschool child. Part I: An experimental study of ascendant behavior in preschool children (University of Iowa Studies in Child Welfare, Vol. IX, No. 3). University of Iowa, 1934.
24. KARSTEN, A. Psychische Sättigung. Psychologische Forschungen, 10:142–254 (1928).
25. LEONTIEV, A. N. The development of voluntary attention in the child. Journal of Genetic Psychology, 40:52–83 (1932).
26. LEUBA, C. J. An experimental study of rivalry in young children. Journal of Comparative Psychology, 16:367–78 (1933).
27. ———. A preliminary analysis of the nature and effect of incentives. Psychological Review, 37:429–40 (1930).
28. LEWIN, K. A dynamic theory of personality. McGraw-Hill Co., New York, 1935. ix + 286 pp.
29. MALLER, J. B. Cooperation and competition: an experimental study in motivation (Teachers College Contributions to Education, No. 384). 1929.
30. MARGINEANU, N. Professor Lewin's conception of laws. Journal of General Psychology, 12:397–415 (1935).
31. MARSTON, L. R. The emotions of young children (University of Iowa Studies in Child Welfare, Vol. III, No. 3). University of Iowa, 1925.
32. MILES, K. A. Sustained visual fixation of preschool children to a delayed stimulus. Child Development, 4:1–5 (1933).
33. MOORE, E. S. The development of mental health in a group of young children: an analysis of factors in purposeful activity (University of Iowa Studies in Child Welfare, Vol. IV, No. 6). University of Iowa, 1931.
34. PALMER, G. Persistence of young children at simple and difficult tasks. Unpublished M. A. thesis, University of Iowa, 1926.
35. PHILIP, BROTHER. The measurement of attention. Unpublished dissertation, Catholic University of America, 1928.
36. ———. Reaction times of children. American Journal of Psychology, 46:379–96 (1934).
37. POYNTZ, L. The efficacy of visual and auditory distractions for preschool children. Child Development, 4:55–72 (1933).
38. SHACTER, H. S. Intelligence as a causal factor determining differences in sustained attention in preschool children. Journal of Applied Psychology, 17:478–88 (1933).
39. ———. A method for measuring the sustained attention of preschool children. Journal of Genetic Psychology, 42:339–71 (1933).
40. ———. Personality tendencies and sustained attention in preschool children. Journal of Social Psychology, 5:313–28 (1934).
41. TAYLOR, C. A comparative study of visual apprehension in nursery school children and adults. Child Development, 2:263–71 (1931).
42. THOMSON, G. H. A formula to correct for the effect of errors of measurement on the correlation of initial values with gains. Journal of Experimental Psychology, 7:321–24 (1924).
43. THORNDIKE, E. L. The influence of the chance imperfections of measures upon the relation of initial score to gain or loss. Journal of Experimental Psychology, 7:225–32 (1924).
44. TOLMAN, E. C. Purposive behavior in animals and men. Century Co., New York, 1932. xiv + 463 pp.
45. YOUNG, P. T. Motivation of behavior. John Wiley and Sons, New York, 1936. xviii + 562 pp.
46. ZUBIN, J. Some effects of incentives: a study of individual differences in rivalry (Teachers College Contributions to Education, No. 532). 1932.

INDEX